The original "bargain mansion"—where creativity took root and, more importantly, where we built a family. It's perfectly imperfect and I couldn't love it more.

Laid-Back
Luxe
YIDDISH WISDOM
the stylist's guide to

Luxe

HOW TO CREATE ASPIRATIONAL AND ATTAINABLE LIVING SPACES

TAMARA DAY

Host of *Bargain Mansions*,
as seen on HBO Max, Magnolia, and HGTV

Countryman Press

An Imprint of W. W. Norton & Company
Independent Publishers Since 1923

Printed in Malaysia
First Edition

For information about special discounts for bulk purchases, please contact W. W. Norton Special Sales at specialsales@wwnorton.com or 800-233-4830

Manufacturing through Imago
Book design by Allison Chi
Production manager: Devon Zahn

Countryman Press
www.countrymanpress.com

An imprint of W. W. Norton & Company, Inc.
500 Fifth Avenue, New York, NY 10110
www.wwnorton.com

978-1-68268-937-0

1 2 3 4 5 6 7 8 9 0

For my family

Contents

Introduction

When I was growing up, my family moved house all the time. My dad, Ward, spent every spare minute improving our latest home and every spare dollar on building materials, trim, or a new shade of paint. As soon as he finished, he sold the house, and we moved again, leaving each house looking a little grander than how we found it.

Years later, I did the same. In 2008, my husband, Bill, and I bought what I would call a bargain mansion. We had just had our third son, and it felt beyond exciting to renovate the sprawling, falling-to-bits Tudor Revival in Kansas City. After moving around so much as a kid, I determined to stay put and make this house our forever home.

But within a few months, the Great Recession hit, and everything changed. Like everyone else, we suddenly had to put our plans on ice. Bill focused on his day job in financial planning, and I stepped in to project-manage the renovation. The house had incredible potential, but it needed a lot of work—and I mean a *lot*. We spent months tearing down rotting walls, sanding floors, and filling in the ~~swamp~~ pool. At one point, I was ripping off wallpaper with a baby strapped to my back and the others crawling around the playpen.

To keep costs down, I thrifted furniture, buying items at estate sales. If something didn't look or feel quite right, I restored or updated it myself. In those first few summers, my three boys, Henry, Bobby, and Thomas (with Nora, our daughter, arriving later), played in the driveway, while I primed and painted old cabinets and coffee tables, swapped hardware, taught myself how to upholster, and we all had fun. (We spent so much time out there that, as a family, we became known as the Driveway Days!) Soon, a friend wanted to buy one of my pieces, then another, and my first commissions came. That momentum gave me the courage to take it a step further, so I launched a series of market days at our home, starring local designer-makers, my vintage furniture, a food truck, and—eventually—a line down the driveway. I loved every moment of it.

Those market days marked a turning point. So many of my first design clients had visited my home already and had seen my style up close. More and more hired me for design projects, which led to founding my own firm. Back when I was sanding floors, if you'd told me that all that wood dust would turn into *Bargain Mansions*, my TV show, I would have laughed, but that's just what happened. I signed a deal and started flipping homes by going to the most up-and-coming neighborhoods, finding the best worst-looking house, and transforming it on camera, against the clock. Six seasons later, with an updated format, I'm still renovating and redecorating the homes of others.

There's one idea that I hold in my mind when I take on a new project. It underlines everything I do: home.

Those early days of 2008 felt so tough, but fire sharpens steel, as they say. If we hadn't lived through the financial crash and if I hadn't approached problems with sledgehammer in hand, my design business and *Bargain Mansions* might never have happened.

I'm proudly self-taught, and though my style has developed over the years, my core principles have stayed the same. To me, the best, most inviting homes—from the smallest studio apartments to rambling mansions—feel unpretentious, optimistic, and have an element of opulence, a style that I call laid-back luxe. **This book will help you create your own version of that feeling.** It contains a celebration of some of my favorite projects, with all the big ideas and smaller, time-saving tips learned along the way.

I'll show you how to create curb appeal and lead you through the home, space by space, with ideas, inspiration, and a little behind-the-scenes know-how. I want to make you feel confident enough to do it yourself and experiment. Instinct and feeling things out powered so much of my early work. Something caught my eye, set my mind whirring, and I had to explore its design possibility. Did it all go smoothly? Nope. Did I have fun and learn how to hone my own style? A hundred percent.

There's one idea that I hold in my mind when I take on a new project. It underlines everything I do: home. It's also a feeling and mood, a place where you share life's important moments with those you love, where you truly feel like yourself, where you recharge. Beautiful, functional design makes life prettier, easier, and better, transforming your day-to-day life and others'. It can feel messy and unpredictable, look funny (ha-ha, weird, or both), or bring tears to your eyes. No matter your style, your home should become the ultimate place to find comfort, inspiration, love, and joy. That's what laid-back luxe means to me.

We're gonna break some RULES.

1 EXTERIORS

CREATE STYLISH, CONSIDERED FACADES

Tudor Revivals with hanging ferns, vintage Craftsman with herringbone pathways, and midcentury masterpieces with blousy hydrangeas—I love them all. For me, the outside of a home matters just as much as the inside. From my years of assessing properties for *Bargain Mansions*, flipping them, and renovating or redesigning the much-loved homes of clients, I've learned that eye-catching exteriors aren't just for others to enjoy. Your home needs to feel uniquely yours. It's not about what everybody else thinks.

When I renovated my own house, a 1980s Tudor Revival, I wasn't designing for guests who might come over once or twice a year. I created it for the people who live there, who call it home: me and my family (the pickiest clients of all!). All my exterior transformations use the same approach. After a long day, as you pull up to your home, you should *feel* that feeling: sweet relief, happiness, and pride in where you live, with a front yard and facade full of your personality.

Most of us want a big update on a small budget [raises hand]. Back then, I was hoping for something to modernize my house while celebrating its roots. In other words, I needed to work *with it* rather than against it—and without breaking the bank. On my TV show and in my property development practice, I've sketched out, sourced, and installed exteriors on all kinds of budgets, from modest to eye-watering. Every one of them strategically used paint, all-season planting, and even a little hog wire. When the budget allowed, new siding, windows, and a deck helped achieve a look that's 100 percent laid-back luxe.

CLASSIC HOUSE STYLES

And How to Refresh Them

Exteriors can tell you a lot about what to expect inside. Is the house a Craftsman, Tudor Revival, or French Provincial? Is it a 1930s bungalow, a 1950s ranch house, or a modern megamansion? Like many cities and towns, the greater Kansas City area has a range of gorgeous (and not so gorgeous) housing stock and styles. As a designer, I've dealt with pretty much all of them and an endless variety of architectural features. More than anything else, the style of a home informs what I want to do with the exterior and interior design. Some clever tricks can make the most of any style.

Craftsman

These architectural icons—small, low, charming stand-alone houses and bungalows—date to the turn of the 20th century. Their exteriors often feature rich detail: low pitched roofs and eaves that overhang wide porches, with gable detailing, sash windows, and wood, *so much wood*. They're just charming. **Underline those historic details by creating color contrasts**, dark navy shingles or siding and white woodwork perhaps, **to refresh these simple structures and make them sing**.

A slightly fancier cousin of the Craftsman, the Shirtwaist style proved most popular in Kansas City. These delightful homes have a sturdy brick or limestone first story with wood-lap siding on the second and third floors. The contrast between the two apparently looks like a tucked-in shirt (and who am I to argue?). Slightly smaller than their mansion neighbors, they have a delightful, vintage feel. **Restoring stonework, highlighting detailing, and some clever planting will do most of the work for you.** Here, a bold pop of coral pink on the front door and porch ceiling adds color to an exterior in a smart, slightly understated way, plus Southern-style ceiling fans and swing seats that my boys helped me build.

before

after

Tudor Revival

This style thrived from the late 1890s to the 1920s and has had many mini-revivals over subsequent decades. Think red brick downstairs, exposed timbering with stone or stucco upstairs, and a sharply sloped roof . . . or three. The design lends itself to a variety of updates. **Highlight the distinctive timbering or hide it in a tonal color scheme.**

For my own home, I added black siding for contrast and copper-toned downspouts for detail (more on that later). This charming Tudor looked weighed down by a tired, 1990s coffee-and-cream color scheme. Driving by, you wouldn't have noticed it. A fresh white highlights the timbers and windows, while a rich, warm gray contrasts with the brick and stucco. Restoring the Craftsman-style, carved front door gave the look a sense of rural realness—and who doesn't want that?

Classic Ranch

These midcentury architectural gems sprang up in suburban neighborhoods, peaking in the 1950s, and still evoke the American West with a simple structure and open interiors. Long, lowdown ramblers, they almost always have one story, with a low roof and garage at the front. Developers and real estate agents have coined several terms to describe the subtle differences among substyles. The Raised Ranch has a split-level layout, and California Ranches have a U- or L-shaped footprint and usually a pool. They all look gorgeous to me. **Add a level**—which, strictly speaking, turns your home into a two-story rather than a ranch—**reclaim space from the garden, or strengthen the connection between the house and outside space with outdoor eating areas, a deck, or similar**.

Colonial

Think simple, rectangular box–shaped houses with two or three stories, dramatically pitched roofs, and often a wooden facade and a gorgeously clunky chimney or two for those inviting fireplaces inside. True Colonials date to English settlements of the 1600s, but contemporary Colonial Revivals often look just as pretty. With a centralized front door and large multipaned windows, the symmetry is easy on the eye—just like French Provincial styles (page 9). These breathtaking, picture-perfect houses up and down the Eastern Seaboard? Colonial house heaven. **Add traditional planting, such as peonies, dark shrubs, and hydrangeas, and a luxe front door.**

Contemporary

Modern houses often (but not always) borrow a little from classic styles, but in general, they behave like a wildcard in terms of design. Modern housing tends to have more open-plan interiors, neutral colors, and traditional materials in the decor. They usually are more sustainable, energy efficient, and accessible than historic houses and usually need only a mild refresh. But creative floor plans sometimes mean that not all Contemporary builds function as well as they could. If you can't influence a layout at the blueprint stage, **increase functionality by improving or redirecting the path from garage to kitchen, redirecting sidewalks, and improving access to the rear**.

Victorian

As the railroads rolled slowly across America, Victorian-style suburban homes sprang up in the mid- to late 1800s; then, in the early 1900s, the Queen Anne style continued its influence. Found in historical city districts as fancy row houses, these asymmetrical houses teem with romantic detailing and might have open porches, balconies, Dutch gables, shingles, tiles, and even towers and dreamy overhanging eaves. They offer lots of visual interest that goes big on craftsmanship. **A color scheme with soft but noticeable contrasts highlights these incredible details.**

Spanish Colonial Revival

From Florida to the West Coast, this style, popular in the early 1900s, draws from traditional Spanish architecture most common around 500 years ago: white stucco walls, clay tile roofs, slightly smaller multipaned windows, discreet columns, rounded arches, and—if intact—gorgeous, hand-carved, heavy wooden front doors. This charming style perfectly suits hot climates. If you have to replace period details lost to time, **these simple, solid structures easily can take a touch of the modern**: new windows, for instance. *¡La casa bonita!*

Farmhouse

Summer trips to my grandparents' farm remain some of my favorite childhood memories, so the traditional American farmhouse has a soft spot in my heart. With wood siding, large windows with black frames, gable roofs, and covered porches, it's a charming style, and contemporary versions look great, too. Rustic, folksy, and rambling, it can be updated easily with a characterful color scheme or refreshed with muted tones. **Retaining those black-framed windows gives a considered, elegant look**, a style note that works well on almost all other architectural styles.

Italianate

From charming row houses to stunning stand-alone mansions, Italianate-style homes draw from traditional architecture in the Italian countryside, but romanticize it with arty detailing from the ancient world: columns, square towers, porches, and irregular shapes. With low roofs and long, slim windows, the best examples date to the mid- to late 1800s, but the style remains prevalent in later builds. Some of these quirky, fascinating homes have a fairy-tale tower, which I love. **Calm, overly ostentatious exteriors with muted colors and soft planting.**

French Provincial

This style has lovely symmetry. The simple, elegant exteriors feel considered, and their lateral footprint impresses—but they can feel flat. When updating an exterior, don't miss the opportunity to add dimension. Just as in good photography, **account for depth and add some interesting angles**.

This French-style house looked dire before renovation. Almost everything needed replacing and modernizing. But the exterior looked charming, and the half-moon arches above the full-length French windows in the main living space made it feel like a fairy-tale ballroom. The huge shutters, the amazing marble fireplace, I wanted to keep it all. On the exterior, we replaced all the windows, refinished them, and applied fresh paint to the shutters, which refreshed the facade. Formal landscaping restored the front yard, echoing the symmetry of the house.

before

after

FRONT DOOR

First Impressions

Is anything more inviting than a great-looking front door? When we first moved into our home, we inherited a classic 1980s front door. It had etched glass and flouncy ribbon detailing and looked *hideous*, but my budget didn't have the wiggle room to replace it. So I worked around it. A great big knocker covered some of the dated detailing. The glass panels came out, and a trim carpenter replaced them with wood paneling. Staining the whole thing made it look good and lasted until we could afford to replace it.

To update yours with a fresh new color, plan for good weather, start early, take the door off its hinges, and prepare to rehang late at night or to sleep with a temporary one. You can paint the door in place, but plan your second coat for the following day. Trust me, it'll take longer than you think! **Dress up your work with thrifted door accessories**—knobs, knockers, house numbers, old-style letter boxes—**or a custom kickplate**.

DECOR

Paint It Black

My house was a fixer-upper, that's for sure—trash-strewn rooms, a colony of wild cats, and a small pool that had turned into a swamp—but those headaches made it the perfect house to renovate! The amount of rotten trim work and broken stucco meant that adding siding to the exterior solved a lot of problems, and it completely changed the look of the home, especially at the rear. Instead of highlighting the Tudor timbering, we went tonal with black paint, no alternative color, just all black. It felt like I tested every color at Sherwin-Williams before landing on Iron Ore, but it still looked a little too brown. Reducing the maroon in it created the perfect bespoke tone. The night after the painters started painting, I lost a lot of sleep, wondering whether I had made a mistake. It felt so bold! But after the house was finished—with copper-colored gutters, pops of red brick, and the beginnings of a garden—it looked timeless and considered.

Finding the perfect paint color always feels like such a challenge, and even more seems at stake when painting an exterior. By way of contrast, **black tones draw attention to natural hues**, including beautifully weathered red brick, warm wood timbers, pale stone, or fresh, green planting. **The little bit of paint that you need to change the color of a door can make a huge difference in your home's first impression.**

My first-ever bargain mansion!

Paint color: Shermin Williams Iron Ore (with less maroon)

PORCH

Make Room

During the demo phase of a renovation, I often **remove elements that make a house feel overdesigned and dated**. A lot of houses are trying to be something they're not, such as a modest home with a modern facade and giant, classical columns on the porch. Something like that just doesn't make sense. Those columns aren't giving bygone Kansas, they're giving ancient Greece!

Consider features that vibe with your house style, and make the most of your porch (if you have one) with seating and accessories for when visitors are waiting for you to answer the doorbell or a nice spot to put a cozy bench and basket. **Increase natural light with windows, a glass pane in your door, or add soft downlights for visual interest.** Planters, a new welcome mat, and a fresh lick of paint go a long way.

Smaller Spaces

If you live in an apartment, consider placing a small side table with a potted plant or seasonal decorative basket outside your front door. If your building restricts repainting or attaching items to your front door, consider hanging small decorative items from the peephole or doorknob, to add a warm, personal touch.

Storage Solution

If you have room on your porch, add a small storage bench where you can keep a garden hose, an extra pair of garden gloves, empty flowerpots or bird baths in winter, and other exterior items that you don't want cluttering a garage or basement.

ACCESSORIES

Thrifted Things

This strategy works great for tight budgets. At an estate sale, thrift store, flea market, or yard sale, you never know what treasures you'll find, and that thrills me! The interior of my home has many thrifted gems, but consider buying some for the exterior also. **Use an old sink as a raised planter, an umbrella stand as a pot for ferns, or an old soup terrine for seasonal cuttings on a table.** Get weird!

This old pony trough lives again as both a water feature and kids' paddling pool.

Metallics contrast well with ceramics.

I love this pig planter; staring up to the sky.

I have a thing for ceramics: the weirder, the better.

Antique ink wells make excellent bud vases.

One of my fave finds: a stone lion's head planter.

Vintage terracotta for potting herbs.

PLANTS AND DESIGN

Ditch Perfection and Walk on the Wild Side

So many of us approach the exterior of a home, the front yard, and even potted plants on the front steps with perfection in mind—as if we must design and maintain it so it looks perfect *all the time*. If you're renovating and restoring, you want the work to look as good as possible, sure, but aiming for strict perfection isn't fun. In Colorado, at a roadside shack, I once found a huge rose quartz boulder. It took three men to load it into my minivan. It sits in my front yard now, it's very, very weird—and I love it.

When it comes to landscaping and outside spaces, I'm all about *im*perfect. Front yards are for looking at *and* for living and playing in, too. **Add a little wildness, something unexpected to break up symmetrical exteriors or just to surprise and delight you and your guests.** If you have a picket-fenced lawn, install some jaw-dropping, Edward Scissorhands–style topiary; desert grasses in simple, understated lines; or a row of billowy hydrangeas. Make it interesting and make it personal.

When walking to the front door, give yourself and others something soft and interesting to look at. For me, that means flowers, shrubs, and trees with different textures and heights. When staging or styling a bookshelf, you don't want all the books and other elements to sit at the same height because that makes them feel regimented and institutional. Not everything has to look symmetrical. If you want to draw attention to your home's exterior symmetry, use asymmetrical elements to frame it. Like a great book, you need good pacing, plus layers of height and depth.

For your exterior space, consider these other questions and ideas.

Think of your home's exterior and front yard like a *giant bookshelf.*

DO YOU WANT STRUCTURE IN YOUR LANDSCAPE? Perhaps you want more of a whimsical look. Pick your plantings accordingly. If you have a more formal exterior, you might plan landscaping in straight lines with traditional boxwoods and lush lawns—or you might play against the formality of that style and do the opposite.

HOW WILL YOUR PLANTS LOOK AS THEY GROW? Will they look good at different stages of growth? Mature perennials give an instant wow, but young, sparser plants still look great with added seasonal blooms to draw the eye. Look for such plants as boxwoods or grasses, which look great at all stages of maturity. Daylilies look great from the get-go. Asparagus might take three to four years to mature, but it looks gorgeous throughout its life. Carrots—yes, in the front yard—give a soft, subtle texture right before harvest time. (Use planters and mesh or chicken wire just underneath the soil's surface, to critter-proof ornamental veggies.)

PLANTING BULBS IN LATE SUMMER TO EARLY FALL ensures a riot of fresh colors in spring, just when you want it most: gladiolus for pinks; amaryllis and fritillaria for reds; daffodils, narcissus, and aconite for yellows; bluebells, crocuses, and irises for purples; hyacinths and snowdrops for whites; and tulips for almost any color you want.

SUMMERTIME CALLS FOR A SALSA POT with cherry tomatoes, peppers, basil, and cilantro all in one planter. Easy and delicious!

The perfect reading-with-a-cocktail spot

PLANTING FOR DECORATION

A Hog-Wire Hack

My home needed something organic and unstructured to soften the formal arch surrounding the porch. At the time, I couldn't afford my first choice: a fancy, custom-fabricated, wrought iron trellis that would have cost thousands. Instead, a roll of hog wire (like giant chicken wire) at a garage sale did the trick for $5. A handyman bent it into a trellis and attached it to the brickwork, and I planted wisteria to the left and right of it. On brick or a dark exterior, a simple wire trellis will all but disappear, and fast-growing creepers or a climbing ivy eventually steals the spotlight. A wonderful, romantic-looking plant, **wisteria quickly adds volume to any exterior**, making it a classic choice. Once planted and happy, it will thrive and grow quickly.

Wisteria bursts into bloom every mid-spring but its soft greenery lasts for months.

Use flowering plants and lush, green cuttings to create arrangements for your outdoor areas. Mismatched pots and thrifted planters give a considered, unique look.

Use your **garden** as a home decor **hack.**

Yes, it's a cliché, but bringing the outside in works for a reason: It's a great idea! My front yard supplies my porch and home with fresh branches, cuttings, and flowers throughout the year. In late fall and throughout the winter, plants and ferns in pretty planters come inside to liven the house. When it's time to cut back dead, seasonal planting, my pruning clippers make quick work of chopping off this and that for going into a wreath or adding branches to an arrangement. That's what I call bringing the outside in.

PATHWAYS

Taking the Right Path

Updating the shape or direction of a path or sidewalk is a game changer. When a house is built, the walk to the front door often just runs in a straight line. Adding a straight line to another straight line doesn't create much interest. You've got a right angle, and that's about it. If your budget allows you to remove it and start from scratch, you can make the pathway much more interesting. A little bit of a curve looks beautiful.

Here are some other tips to liven the path to a more beautiful exterior for your home.

Use **reclaimed bricks** to add texture and color without sacrificing sturdiness.

Pressed concrete allows you to create beautiful custom designs and textures, imprinting it while still wet with a stamp, such as herringbone, without having to spend a fortune on custom masonry.

Rope-lining a sidewalk looks gorgeous, and rope treated with decking oil can last a few wet seasons.

Giant, thick pavers add drama and look great with a little growth in between. If you live in a rainy climate, little strips of faux grass—yes, like AstroTurf—look great.

ESSENTIALS

Porch Must-Haves

If I can add a pair of sconces to a porch or entryway, I will—it's my thing! If you're lucky enough to have a porch or outdoor seating, you have so many ways to create inviting and surprising spaces.

Here's my cheat sheet of other essentials (sconces included, of course).

- Sconces for decorative fun
- Planters for flower power
- Mood lighting for evening atmosphere
- Statement light for a little upscale elegance
- Hog wire as an affordable, folksy, offbeat trellis alternative that's easy to install
- Outdoor rug or graphic welcome mat for a homely, modern touch
- Something weird: a surprising addition to add personality

Home Stories

FROM BRICK TO BEAUTIFUL

This midcentury-style build, a sprawling one-story structure, looked weather-worn and dated—a brick box. It desperately needed some personality and a refresh to reveal its otherwise interesting design. From renovating my own home, I knew that adding black and charcoal tones, a bold move, would give the house renewed focus that the owners would take pride in, and feel excited by, as they arrived home. The transformation amazed even me! Framed by greenery, this chic exterior uses a confidently bright orange front door as a focal point.

Originally, this house faded into the background, hiding its otherwise fascinating midcentury details.

PERFECT BLUE

When I first saw it, this classic Craftsman had zero curb appeal. With a dull brown color scheme, no artful features stood out. It needed a series of contrasts: highlighting the pretty, multipaned windows in a fresh white; adding a perfect blue tone to the wooden shingle exterior; and painting the front door a peony pink. The overall effect was stunning, especially the windows, which now seem larger and more inviting (the power of white paint on a dark background!).

Before my transformation this cute Craftsman was every shade of brown imaginable.

I wanted a playful, contrasting color for the front door and I was tickled pink with the result.

HAVE FUN

It's Allowed!

My interior design and property development business, my TV show, and even my product lines and collaborations all started in my driveway. Restoring interesting pieces of antique and vintage furniture from thrift stores and estate sales—sanding, priming, and painting by hand—transforms them into something new. All that usually takes place in the driveway, so my driveway is the only part of the exterior I haven't improved . . . yet! When my kids were growing up, we all had so much fun out there on the concrete.

Some of my favorite family pictures were taken on that driveway; I'm in a white dress, and the boys are playing hopscotch beside me. When they were really little and I was restoring a piece of furniture, I spray-painted a hopscotch grid for them, which created a great space for them to burn off energy and gave them creative confidence. When I wasn't home, they could get out the spray paint and use it here. Once, they created a H-O-R-S-E ring around our basketball goal. It can feel challenging to live through a renovation, so let off a little steam. About to redecorate your walls? Let the kids scribble on them first or paint a mural there yourself. Write paint color names large across your soon-to-be-transformed living room or get into the detail and prep furniture for your kids to paint for their own bedrooms. A little restraint is good, but allow yourself to have some fun along the way!

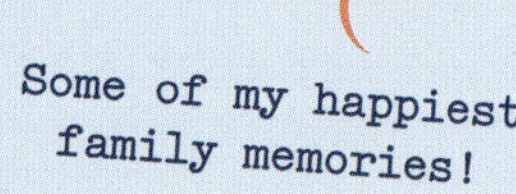

Some of my happiest family memories!

CHECKLIST

- [ ] Identify your house or apartment building style to honor it while making your own updates and clever contrasts to bold and bright, traditional, or contemporary structures. Pay special attention to this transformative aspect.
- [ ] Use soft or strong contrasts to highlight certain details (and hide others).
- [ ] Accessorize with sconces, lighting, and something weird. (Why not?)
- [ ] Revitalize your porch, closing it in, opening it up, adding windows, or a lick of paint.
- [ ] Plant smart. From window boxes to landscaping, don't overlook this essential aspect.
- [ ] Plant decoratively, which you can do affordably and creatively. (Hello, hog wire!)
- [ ] Consider rerouting pathways, repaving, or imprinting a design in new concrete.
- [ ] Have fun! Leave space out front for games and neighbor hangouts.

2 ENTRYWAYS

COME ON IN

What do you do when you first step through your front door? Toss your keys on a table? Kick off your shoes? Kiss loved ones hello? In the entryway, **great design starts with function and ends with a smile**. As a designer, I ask myself, *What's this room's job? What does this space need to do?* But that's just a starting point. Once your entryway works for you—the front door opens easily; there's enough light; and you have somewhere to toss those keys, hang a coat, and kick off those shoes—you can make it magical.

Large homes often have grand entrances and front halls so spacious that they can serve not just as a landing spot but as reading areas and even home offices, with the right design strategies. But I also design smaller homes that often have a well-thought-out (if sometimes dated) entryway, all with smaller entryways—and some with no real entry space at all.

With every home, two main rules apply to this part of the dwelling. First, **entryways must provide good service** to you and whoever shares your home with you: kids, strollers, dogs, plants, whatever. In an apartment, that means a through-space for groceries, trash, even bikes or scooters. Be *brutally* honest with yourself here. If you always put your designer jacket carefully on a hanger before filing it neatly in a closet, well, good for you. But if you're more of a Miranda Priestly coat-dumper, throwing your outerwear in a heap on the hallway table as soon as the front door closes (no judgment), design this space with that habit in mind. Make sure your entryway has enough accessible hooks, shoe storage, or closet space within arm's reach.

Second, **the entryway officially welcomes guests, giving you an opportunity to foster hospitality through design**—and I love that. After people walk through the front door, they see the entryway, so think of it as the first thing on the menu.

Include special details: a large, flattering mirror; beautiful artwork; a surface for keys and mail; fresh flowers or plants; a gorgeous rug; a place to hang coats and store umbrellas; somewhere comfortable to sit; and even something a little weird to draw the eye. In terms of colors, textures, wallpaper, and fabrics, consider the home as a whole. Do you want the entry to echo the rest of the house, or do you want to create contrast for dramatic effect? Do you want to restore period details to shine again, or do you have a blank, boring canvas crying out for a pop of color and a little TLC?

The entryway is the appetizer for your home.

Everyone who passes through your entryway should feel immediately comfortable. (What can I say? It's the Midwest in me. Come over to my place, and it won't be long before you have a drink in one hand and a snack in the other.) If you have company over in the evening, start setting the scene right here. A table lamp or two should be glowing, light a scented candle, and have music playing softly while you're making your guests a delicious drink—beautifully garnished, of course.

Display fresh flowers and stage some interesting objects as talking points, like my pair of porcelain Gucci slides, my something weird. A designer friend took such pride in his first purchase of luxury shoes that, after he had worn them to death, he had his favorite pair of slides cast in porcelain with gorgeous gold highlights. He gifted me one of his early samples. From the moment I set eyes on them, I've loved them, and they've sat in my entryway ever since. Start with function and end with a smile.

WHAT'S YOUR STYLE?

With the existing architectural style of your home in mind, a little inward thinking here will help you discern your style. First, what do you already like? Are you in love with a particular contemporary light fitting or a specific vintage floral wallpaper? Do bright tones draw you, or muted colors? Monochrome modernity or warm wood? Identify what you love and build from there.

Here's a quick quiz to help!

Do you love traditional tones, fine detailing, craftsmanship, and luxurious finishes thoughtfully curated for comfort and elegance? You're an **Old-World Charmer**.

Drawn to playful but considered interiors with bold motifs, natural textures, and muted tones with unexpected juxtapositions and retro, midcentury finds? **Modern Vintage** is your thing.

Excited by everything vibrant and visually rich? Love multipatterned and eclectic with bold tones and uplifting vistas? Are you a bold, anything-goes kind of person? You embrace **Joyful Maximalism**.

Do you prefer more understated style? Do you feel the need for airy and authentic living spaces with clean lines, the best handpicked natural materials, and neutral tones? Confidently simple, discerning, and incredibly calming, this is **Contemporary** style.

Adore luxurious finishes, dark tones, and warm metals (brass, gold)? Drawn to indulgent elements with drama and scale, from the traditional to the modern? This is **New Glamour**.

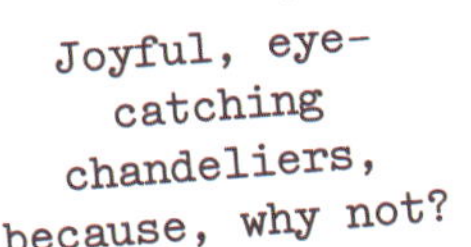

Joyful, eye-catching chandeliers, because, why not?

PALM BEACH
MARVEL

Laid-Back Lexicon

RETRO NEW BUT DESIGNED TO LOOK OLD-FASHIONED

CLASSIC NEW OR OLD BUT TIMELESS

VINTAGE 20 TO 99 YEARS OLD

ANTIQUE 100 OR MORE YEARS OLD

LAYOUT

Add to What You Have

Older properties tend to have less storage. Renovating gives you a chance to increase these areas or to reconfigure them so they work harder for you. **Large, imposing spaces can develop character when you fill some of that space**, responding to the scale with statement lights, art, shelving, and furniture.

No Entryway, No Problem

Open-plan, one-story homes, such as sprawling ranch houses or Contemporary builds, and loft-style or small apartments can open straight into the main living space without much of an entryway at all. With little wall space and no under-the-stairs nooks to fill with built-ins, it might seem like your entryway will need a different design approach, but the principle remains the same. Start with function and end with joy. You still need storage—a set of hooks or a coat stand, a basket for umbrellas, a shelf for shoes—and a surface for smaller essentials. A bold cabinet works well here because it can help delineate the space, and a small rug further defines the area as an entryway. Clever lighting, art, a mirror, flowers, and a dish make sense here, but don't crowd that useful surface area. Rather than a table lamp here, try a pendant light teamed with a pair of sconce lights.

Glass-paned pocket doors can help delineate larger areas.

A simple seating area, a little storage, and something soft—it doesn't have to be complicated.

DECOR

Bloom Time

Fresh flowers are my weakness, and for an entryway arrangement, I go *big*. Oversize cuttings and branches (medium to large) from my garden form the centerpiece of my entryway space. They give a sculptural, slightly insane appearance that always looks beautiful, adding instant drama. Throughout the year, elements change: wildflowers and aromatic herbs, such as basil and fennel tops, in spring and summer; fiery red leaves in fall; berries and evergreens in winter. In December, a tabletop Christmas tree dressed to the nines replaces everything, so my beloved porcelain Gucci slides can rest for a month or so.

Mirror, Mirror

An essential for last-minute fixing lipstick, mussing hair, and straightening clothes.

Hanging Art

If you have walls, you can hang art. Paintings, prints, and photos hung haphazardly, in a grid, or—a great solution for rentals—against the wall on a table or shelf, help set the tone. Mix mediums and styles in art and frames. Arrange artful objects and books on open shelving or a bookcase to showcase your personality further.

In every entryway that I create goes a piece of art or three. (My own has *five*!) The pieces come directly from local artists, estate sales, and a few online marketplaces, for good measure. **Odd numbers—three or five—have a more pleasing, eclectic look than stiffly paired even numbers.** Even if you have limited space, a great piece of art in a stunning frame can make all the difference, and you can rotate pieces to freshen the space instantly.

Use sconces to elevate your artworks.
Paint color:
Sherwin Williams
Mega Greige

Dish It

For your keys and pocket change, matchbooks and stray hair ties, loyalty cards and everything between, consider a marble bowl, a lacquered trinket tray, a candy dish, even a vintage ashtray from someplace like the Chateau Marmont—anything useful that sparks pleasure.

Keep it simple with a sculptural dish for entryway essentials.

Scented spaces create real ambiance.

Delight the Nose

Starting with the entryway, use scented candles and diffusers at strategic points. There's something truly delightful about opening the front door and breathing in an incredible scent that changes as you pass through the different spaces of the home. Citrus and pine scents do it for me, and my absolute favorite fragrance is grapefruit and mint; I love it so much that I designed my own candle version. (It's gorgeous, even if I say so myself.)

Look again: This stack of fluffy towels is actually a ceramic sculpture!

Find Your Weird

The thrift gods have been kind to me, and I have filled houses and homes with fascinating, functional items that draw the eye. Deployed around the home, interesting items from a flea market, thrift store, or estate sale start conversations. Always follow a style that makes sense *of* your space and *in* your space, creating an easy, calming flow throughout your home. But now and again, allow yourself something off the wall. Give yourself permission to add a little personality to your entryway.

STORAGE SOLUTIONS

Put It Away

Storage can feel like one of the least glamorous aspects of home design (and sometimes that's true), but for me, it's one of the most exciting. With clever storage solutions—whether you stow your stuff or arrange it neatly and purposefully in full view—you can take your home design anywhere you like, with few restrictions. In the entryway, storage is king.

If you don't have a closet or room for one, consider built-in cabinetry with large, deep sliding drawers and organizer inserts (perfect for storing little coats, boots, and shoes), a banquette with storage, or freestanding storage benches, plain or upholstered. Even a small chair and storage ottoman can work perfectly. Handpick some out-of-the-ordinary coat hooks (more on that in a moment), thrift a basket or a large tray for shoes and umbrellas, and perhaps create a separate area for dog things, including a vintage cookie jar for treats. If you're short on floor space, place a small table, pot stand, or even a floating shelf at table height here as a great place to drop your keys and the mail.

Paint color: Benjamin Moore Black Forest Green

Hooked on It

If you have limited space with no closet nearby, a set of beautiful, thoughtful hooks or a coatrack can go a long way. This small investment can have high impact. Most people get a set of simple hooks at the hardware store, but that's a missed opportunity. Look for beautiful designs online. Etsy, for example, has fabulous vintage and antique ones. Do a cute mix of different styles or a more structured, formal look. Every home decor store has coat hooks, but **look in the bathroom section for robe hooks**, which run a little beefier and prove more durable.

Many entryways can't handle heavy hooks and the even heavier items (big coats, wet coats, more coats) that hang from them, especially if you have to screw into sheetrock. If you live in a rental or apartment where you can't cut into the wall, use a simple wooden plate—a beautiful solid piece of wood or something inexpensive painted up—attach your hooks to the wood, and secure the plate to the wall studs. It looks great, evenly distributes the weight on the wall, and it's supereasy to undo when you move out.

Paint color: Sherwin Williams Oceanside

LIGHTING

Make a Statement

Most entryways usually look too dark or, overlit from one source with the wrong lightbulbs, way too bright. You easily can remedy both off-putting scenarios. **Add layered lighting design** with table lamps, picture lamps, sconces (hardwired or stuck on and rechargeable), perhaps can lighting in the ceiling, and a statement pendant, all in conversation with one another. Different qualities, tones, and directions of light create rich, visual interest, and a bold chandelier or pendant light that you love unifies the design and looks stunning. Being mindful of light-strength and tone when you purchase bulbs or tweak your lighting can make a huge difference. Just as important as the strength of light are the color of each bulb and the overall system. **2,700 Kelvins look best.**

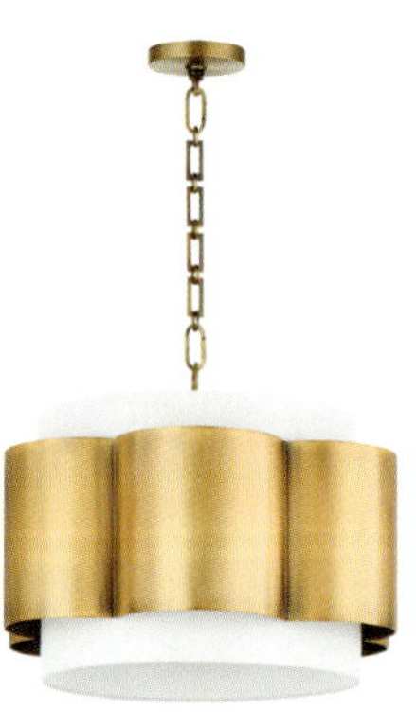

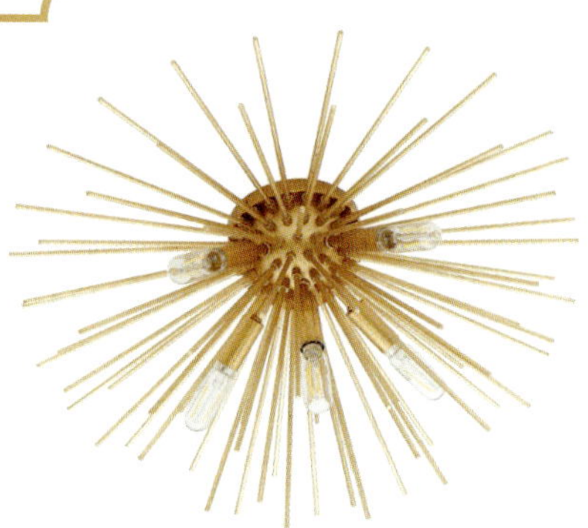

In the right space, soft pink lightbulbs can make you look **fabulous.** They look great close to a mirror and act like rose-tinted glasses for your skin.

FORGOTTEN SPACES

Alternative Entryways

In car country, many of us enter the home through the garage. If you do that 90 percent of the week, this entryway really deserves some thought, too. Spaces like this usually have a behind-the-scenes, purely functional, undesigned feeling because a lot of people design the spaces that *other* people see but not the spaces where they live. But there's an opportunity for fun here! My own garage—full of cars, bikes, and an old Jet Ski—has great lighting, plants in pots on tiered shelving, some interesting and weird objects, and I love driving into it. It's not guest-facing, but it still brings a smile to my face.

For more about how to design this kind of private entryway, see the discussion of mudrooms (page 241).

My own garage for inspiration (old Jet Ski not pictured).

Home Stories

EMBRACING THE OLD

More than 100 years ago, a local fire chief built this historic home for his daughter. Naturally fireproof, it's 100 percent brick. For demo and reno, not having drywall or wooden partitions to play with usually poses a problem, but the brick looked beautiful, so I wanted to embrace that. Even with a big, triple-pane entryway, the low ceiling still made the space look dark, so I brightened it with a warm, multibulb statement light that ran horizontally (rather than vertically, which would have interfered with door swing), added bright artwork, and installed a sliding barn door at the side to conserve space. The driveway lies at the side of the house, and the stairs led to a spot where the original owners could climb into a horse-drawn buggy, a wonderful historic detail.

Wide, short-depth statement lights are perfect for low ceilings.

THE JEWEL BOX

Sometimes, a house truly surprises me. Before my first site visit, the clients said they wanted a *huge* transformation, including changing *every single fixture and fitting*. Their enthusiasm excited me, but the original trim detailing and crystal chandeliers were breathtaking. The family loves bold color, so with the glittering light fitting already in place, I approached this entryway with a jewelry-box theme. (The family agreed to keep the original light, which thrilled me because it's just gorgeous.) Creating a tone story with Tiffany-like blue and a gloss finish and a deeper navy in the room beyond played into the jewel theme.

MIDCENTURY CASTLE

One *Bargain Mansions* building, where comedy legend Bob Hope once stayed as a guest, went from a confused, midcentury Disney castle to a chic, contemporary château, and it all started with this showstopping entryway. The center of the facade looked like a castle turret, with a conical roof ending in a sharp point, and the front door cut through the center of the circular vestibule. The contractor who brought me onto the project almost passed on it because he couldn't imagine it looking good, but that's the kind of situation that gets me excited. Still, the entryway proved challenging. The huge, drafty space resisted obvious solutions. It had no flat walls on which to hang anything, and the vaulted ceiling felt more suited to a church than a home. We moved the inset front door out to the exterior wall, to create a larger vestibule, added a marble table for flowers, and installed five statement pendants, each 2 feet wide and hung at different heights from a false ceiling panel. **Don't be afraid to fill up a space to create your look.**

DESIGNING FOR PERSONALITY

All brick, glass, and tile, this 1960s home with a flat-top roof felt formal and soulless. It was giving sad-office-building vibe. Opening the front door revealed literally the entire house at the same time, which was overwhelming. It needed a discrete entryway so you could stop and appreciate the space. Adding this slatted wood room divider kept the floor plan open but still felt historically accurate along with the orange chair and the Sputnik-style lamp spread along the lower ceiling. We even saved a delightful old rubber plant that had rooted and grown under the foundation of the house. **If you can't change it, embrace it!**

FROM PURPLE HEADACHE TO PALE OAK PARQUET

From the start, this house proved hard to define. Built in the late 1970s or early '80s, it had no discernible era or style. It looked tired and dated, with a dark and unwelcoming entryway behind a set of bright purple front doors. Yet it had incredible potential. The space needed to feel contemporary with some classic touches, a farmhouse quality (because the backyard overlooks a horse ranch), and the youth and sense of fun of the owners. We added a pale oak parquet floor laid in a classic herringbone pattern to point the way into the house. Fresh, bone-colored paintwork and a modern black console anchored the space, and a new set of gorgeous, solid-wood doors with beveled glass flooded the entry with natural light.

In your entryway, use flooring designs, such as a classic herringbone, to point the way for your guests.

You don't need a **big entryway** to make a **big statement.**

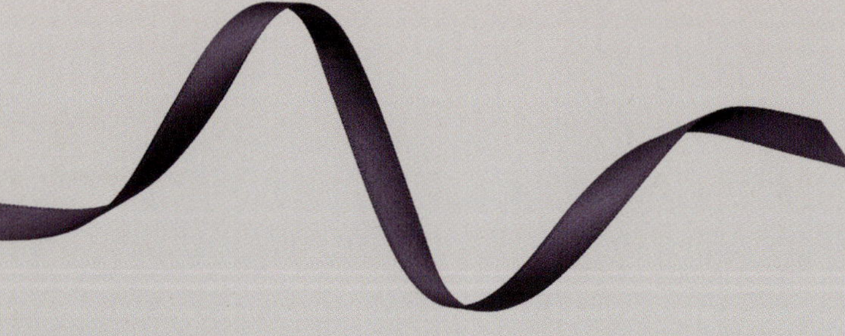

CHECKLIST

- ☐ Use layered lighting and statement pieces.
- ☐ Storage for coats and shoes can range from bespoke cabinetry to vintage hooks and a thrifted basket.
- ☐ If you want to go bold, do it here with wallpaper. Consider oversize florals or midcentury modern graphics.
- ☐ Add a mirror in a whimsical frame. Think modern sculpted metal, ornate gilded plaster, or carved and painted wood.
- ☐ Hang beautiful artwork: a painting, a collection of related prints, even framed needlework.
- ☐ A small table or floating shelf at table height provides a great place to set your keys and mail. You also can stage drinks on it for visitors as they enter.
- ☐ Stage and style your entryway with fresh flowers or plants. Consider including an inviting fragrance element.
- ☐ Even if you want your entry to contrast with the next space in your home, choose a rug that reflects your overall style.
- ☐ Find your weird, add something truly individual, and let your personality shine.

3

LIVING SPACES

LIVING IS EASY

LIVING IN THE LIVING ROOM

The best living rooms feel cohesive and multifunctional and suit many personalities. My house has an official home office (page 165) that I love, but I'm a nomad in real life. On-site for demolition or shooting, I'll set up just about anywhere. At home, my laptop, sketches, and fabric samples follow me all over the house. You'll find me typing at the kitchen counter, in the dining room, on the deck, in bed when the weather's gray and cold, but mostly in the living room. It's the most comfortable, quietly inspiring space in the home, and it works just as hard as my sometime office, a hangout area for the family, and even a cocktail corner before dinner with friends.

You can use many tricks and hacks to make your living space worth living in: hanging good art, delineating zones with rugs, and adding a reading or meditation nook, for example. But first, let's be honest: How much time are you going to spend here? Do you always gravitate here, as comfortable hosting a gathering as you are hunkering under a blanket with a scary movie playing?—or back in the day, would you have called this space the "good" room, with carefully presented objects, a sofa covered in plastic, and a rarely walked-on carpet? Perhaps you need an occasional dining area, room for a yoga mat, or a dog bed for a Great Dane? **Really think about how you're going to use the space.** *Before* you renovate or redecorate, recognize how you use it. What works, and what doesn't?

For my home and most of the houses I've worked on, the room needs versatility, which informs almost everything that follows: placement of art in relation to TV—or no TV at all (more on that later), flooring and lighting, furnishings, occasional tables and other surfaces, and stylish storage. First, nail down these details (not literally); then you can get to the fun part: expressing your aesthetic, choosing the perfect sofa, using soft furnishings to transition your space throughout the day, and creating a perfect place to spend your time.

LIGHTING

Going Big and Bold

As in almost every other space, layered lighting from multiple sources works perfectly here. With warm-toned bulbs in lamps, sconces, and statement pendants, **layered lighting gives depth and a variety of focal points, and it looks glorious.** Choose breathtakingly huge pendants: vintage blown glass, crystal chandeliers, modern masterpieces, or even some of my own creations. For a statement light, the bigger the better. Smaller pendants look great in hallways and by beds (page 189), and the trend is heading steadily toward bold, magnificent color, design, and texture, which I love.

Pro Tip

Layered lighting is particularly important for neurodivergent people: Add dimmers where possible and avoid overly harsh lights that tend to flicker. Consider lighting for specific tasks, deal with those annoying shadows in work areas, and try to create a tailored-to-you system that is functional, calming and, most importantly, gorgeous.

LAYOUT

Designing for Conversation

When planning the placement of a sofa, armchairs, other seating, coffee tables, side tables, or a bar cart styled to the nines (page 74), pay attention to spacing. **Measure the room and tape out on the floor where you want place the pieces.** Think about how you'll move through the room, the pathways you'll take to other spaces, and even the view from various seats. Seating needs to feel comfortable enough and close enough for people to communicate, so create a space conducive to chatting. If you're lucky enough to have a giant room and your couches sit too far apart for people to chat, that's going to make for awkward conversation. Also, **your couch doesn't have to go against a wall**.

Will everybody want to slump together on a sectional with a built-in chaise? If so, consider shared seating over one that favors personal space. That arrangement might not feel right if you mostly are entertaining friends here, rather than hanging out with family. In that case, two or three smaller pieces will work well.

Smaller Spaces

In an ideal world, the living room should have two identical sofas facing each other and two chairs flanking them. If your space doesn't allow for that much furniture, go for one sofa and two chairs facing a central coffee table as a space-saving alternative. For less room than that, three or four club chairs around a table save space but still will keep the conversation rolling. In a supersmall room, opt for one loveseat with a padded ottoman or tuck some padded stools under a console or side table, for extra seating.

SOFA STYLES

Laid-Back Lexicon

Designers and manufacturers sometimes use different style names. Here are the most popular styles and silhouettes that you should know.

Chaise longue (not lounge), usually has one arm and allows one person to recline with feet up. It's perfect for small, unexpected spaces. Think of it as the original "design" chair: not totally practical, but a luxurious addition and gorgeous to behold.

Couch, intended for lounging and even napping, feels more casual than a **sofa** and doesn't always have arms.

In midwestern and mid-Atlantic America, a **davenport** usually means a couch.

Divan, a backless day bed, sits low to the ground, usually against a wall. Lots of pillows provide comfort and support.

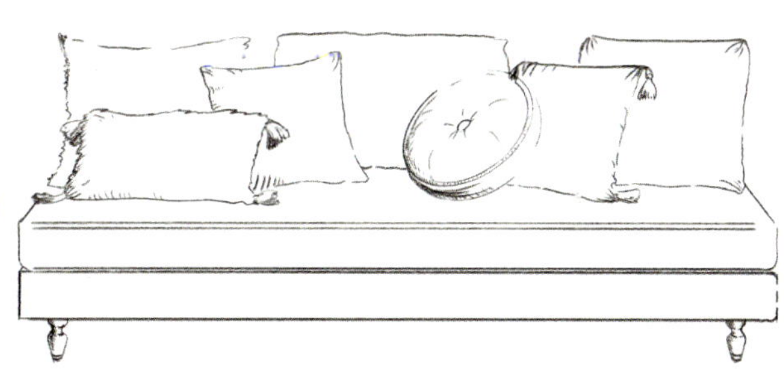

Loveseat, usually more comfortable than a **settee**, fits just two people.

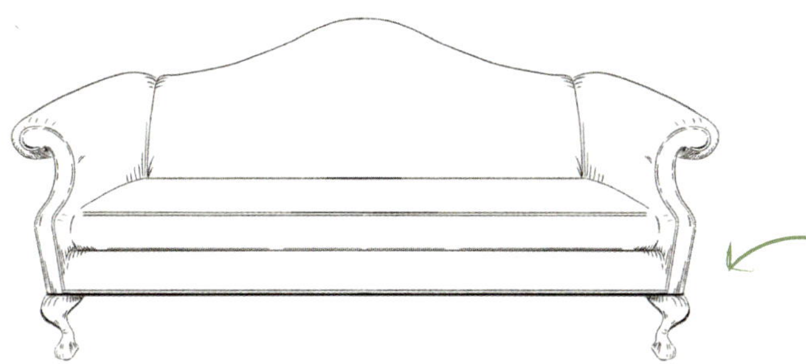

Sofa, looks more formal and has more structure than a **couch**.

The **camelback** or humpback sofa, a quirky relative of the **English roll arm**, has a stylistic raised back and wooden legs.

The classic tufted **chesterfield**, a traditional design with a clubhouse vibe, looks good anywhere; firm but deep and usually (but not always) upholstered in leather. Finding good-quality, vintage examples of this style is like panning for gold, but modern interpretations offer upscale perfection.

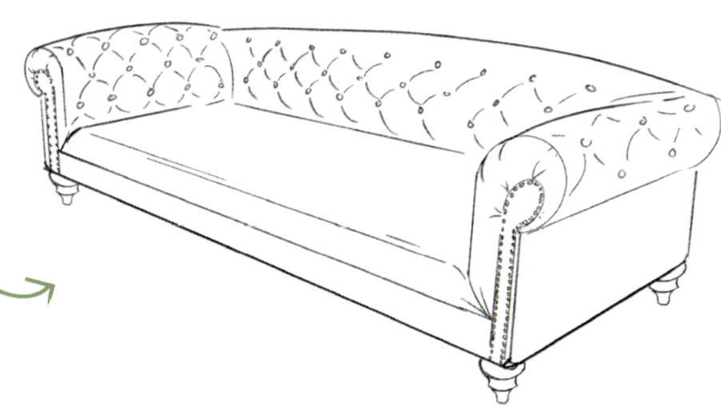

The delightful **English roll arm** needs a little extra space for its angled-out armrests and firm, high back. Its old-world charm works well in comfortable, homely, eclectic spaces, rather than super-modern, minimalist environments.

Many of us rarely go farther than the **Lawson**, and with good reason. It's the ultimate classic couch shape and the king of goes-with-anything, easy comfort. I'm a fan.

The **midcentury modern** sofa looks clean and minimal, with right angles, a high back, slightly shorter legs so it sits lower to the ground, and a simple, slightly retro aesthetic overall.

Sectional, the most versatile style, gives you multiple layout configurations (L, U, and so on). Because it comes in sections, it can be the best option for apartment buildings and homes with narrow entryways.

Settee, a small, traditional two-seater, smaller and more formal than a **loveseat**, works hard in small spaces, especially in dual formation. Its upright design can make it a great addition to larger spaces as secondary seating, or it might fit perfectly in a nook or hallway where people won't be sitting for a long time.

Tuxedo, a simple, elegant style, all boxy right angles, has arms and back of equal height and occasionally features tufting for a little detail. It looks great in modern, open-plan living.

How to Choose Your Forever Sofa

When dreaming of and designing your living space, think of seating and your sofa(s) as an investment. Good-quality, durable pieces covered in good fabric or upholstery will last almost forever—or at least long enough that you'll tire of your couch before it tires of you.

Buying a sofa feels like a huge commitment, so **let your butt do the choosing**. Do you like something firm with a tall back to support upright posture? If so, go for a well-structured midcentury-style piece. Do you love to curl into something lowdown, soft, and marshmallowy? Sofas with loose cushions can look sunken and slouchy and might need frequent straightening. If you don't want to keep fluffing pillows, opt for a sectional with a chaise. For smaller spaces, go for a one-piece, a sectional for bespoke formations, a pair of loveseats or settees, or just one.

Don't forget to consider the arms. Will you use them to balance drinks? Will guests sit on them during a big get-together? What will your pet(s) think? Does the sofa need to survive cat claws or dog slobber? Here's a great way to test the longevity of a particular style or brand. Look it up on resale sites to see whether it has worn well. Chairish and Kaiyo offer more upscale, quality preloved pieces, but also try Instagram, Facebook Marketplace, eBay, and even Craigslist. The auctioneer 1stDibs offers rare, antique, and contemporary designs, with a price tag to match.

For fabrics, narrow your options to soft, inviting, and easy-to-care-for materials because high-maintenance cleaning is never fun. Think chenille, cotton velvet, or marine canvas. On upholstered pieces, consider mixing materials, such as chairs with leather seats and fabric bodies.

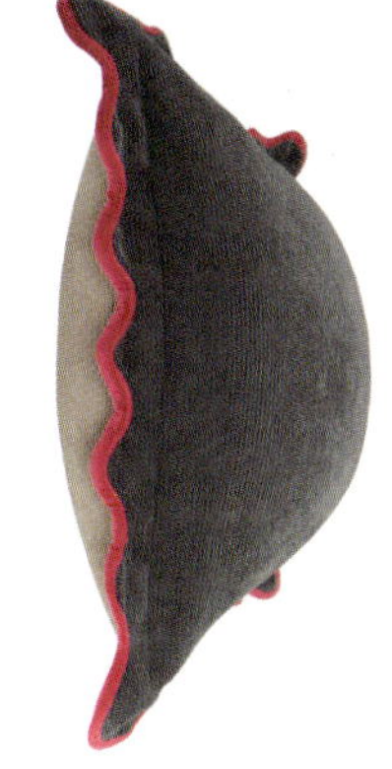

SOFT STUFF

Transitioning Your Space from Day to Night

More of us work from home than ever, which means that many living spaces need to function as a daytime break room, impromptu yoga studio, evening gathering area, *and* a cozy space to hang out under a blanket with a rom com playing in the background. **To transition a living space throughout the day, use soft furnishings:** floor cushions, pillows, and blankets. When a new mood strikes or need arises, these elements move or rearrange so easily, and all add to the overall design. Throws can live on certain chairs and armrests, giant bolsters and large floor cushions can emerge from storage (page 78) as extra seating, and extra pillows also can hide until needed. **Stage a blanket hierarchy in a basket:** prettiest blanket on top and the cozy but less photogenic ones underneath.

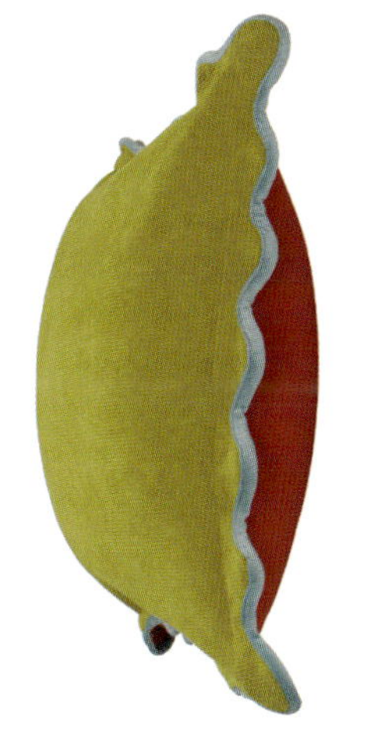

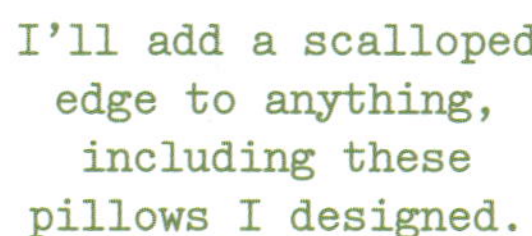
I'll add a scalloped edge to anything, including these pillows I designed.

HANGING ART

Instantly Transform Your Living Space

The right art can transform your living space, but committing to hanging that perfect piece can feel nerve-racking. Abstract pieces allow you to riff on their colors and textures, echoing or adding to the color story of a space. Photography and portraits also work well. Displaying an eclectic collection throughout the home often looks more interesting than different iterations of the same kind of art. **Match the size and style of the artwork with the aesthetic of the space.** Do you want to showcase a single, bold statement piece in the center of lots of negative space; to assemble a cozy, artsy atmosphere with a gallery wall of smaller, mismatched pieces; or to create a structured grid with a series of framed works?

For individual pieces, **aim for eye level, 57 to 60 inches from the floor**. Your art will thank you for it. If you're assembling a gallery wall, use the same measurement either to center a simple grid or to baseline an intentionally haphazard collection. Mix and match sizes, orientations, and frames to create something unique. Try different configurations by sketching them on paper or laying them on the floor until you find the arrangement that you love. **Before you hang anything, use one or more cardboard cutouts that match the dimensions of whatever you want to hang.** Tape each cutout lightly in place to confirm that you like where it will hang on the surface *and* in relation to surrounding elements.

For informal, unframed works, use poster hangers. For lightweight pieces, go with wall hooks. For anything midweight, use standard picture hangers. Wall anchors with screws work best for heavier pieces.

SCREEN TIME

What to Do with the TV?

Lots of people argue about whether to have a TV in the living room, and I'm not going to pick a side because I understand both positions. For the first 15 years in our home, we didn't have a TV in our main living space. When the Kansas City Chiefs announced a big game, we invited friends over to watch. Everyone said yes, the Chiefs won, the event snowballed, and soon we regularly were hosting a crowd of 60 with borrowed screens across three rooms. It was so much fun that we finally installed a television in the living room. (It took me two weeks to learn how to turn it on!)

If you do want a TV in this space, finding ways of incorporating it nicely, matching the scale of the room. The screen can live anywhere comfortable to look at. (Head to page 152 for tips on perfect screen placement.) Fine-framed TVs, with matte-look screens and the ability to display digital artwork, can look great. But if you have the inclination and the space, including somewhere else that you like to watch TV, consider keeping your living room free from electronics, to encourage conversation and interaction.

Make a feature of your TV by balancing it with other black elements.

DESIGN IDEAS

Welcome to the Inspiration

Hotel design fascinates me. So much of my inspiration comes from the grand lobbies and hallways of the old classics as well as the lounges and moody cocktail corners of modern masterpieces, cute bespoke inns, and even vacation rentals. Really good hotels either have gorgeous interiors that have stood the test of time or showcase some of the most creative, mindful design ideas out there. They just *work*.

The best places to stay often use a mindful approach to space with clever, sometimes unexpected touches like the lobby of the Inn at Meadowbrook, a gorgeous sprawling hotel in Prairie Village, near Kansas City, pictured here. If you spot something that interests you or that you love—groups of chairs, a bistro table inside a suite, a fireside sofa, a velvet booth, benches around a pillar—take a quick photo. (Not all your travel photos have to be beach selfies, iconic landmarks, or scenic landscapes.) These smaller design moments add up and can kick-start connection back home. If you like where you're staying, make it a learning moment!

INVESTING IN VALUE

Being Honest with Your Budget

If you're going to spend significant time in your living room. Consider those big annual events, parties and such, sure, but **don't design an everyday space for once-a-year occasions**. If you're going to be there every day, make it a room you love and invest in it accordingly.

BREAD

How to Style Any Room

Here's my tried-and-tested, Tamara Day formula for styling almost any space:

- **CANDLES AND BOOKS**
  belong in every room. After that, add:

- **SOMETHING BLACK**
  to anchor the room;

- **SOMETHING OLD**
  for subtlety and character;

- **SOMETHING WOOD**
  to add warmth and tone;

- **SOMETHING ALIVE,**
  including potted plants, cuttings, or flowers to liven the space;

- **SOMETHING SOFT,**
  such as a rug, a pillow, or a comfy blanket to signify comfort; and

- **SOMETHING WEIRD**
  to draw the eye. Trust me on this one!

Whether new or vintage and reclaimed, bar carts offer lots of opportunities for gorgeous design. Here's my foolproof method for turning a bar cart into a showstopper.

- **Start with the basics:** beautiful bottles (full or empty), glassware, and tools. Buy beautiful glassware that will last you years. You can thrift it so easily, and it's decor you can use! A variety of heights and styles will add good variation.
- **Group like items together** on trays or even beautiful cocktail books lying flat.
- **Create balance by arranging items by height**, so tall items, such as bottles and decanters in the back or on one side, and shorter items, including shakers and glasses in the front or on the other side.
- **Add greenery.** No space is complete without fresh flowers or a plant, and the same goes for a bar cart. One word: garnish!
- **Add a couple of accessories that represent your personality**, such as fun cocktail napkins, coasters, candlesticks, this book (wink, wink), or small piece of artwork.

FLOORING

From Natural to Almost Natural

The living space has relatively low traffic and a low risk of spills, so you can install truly luxurious flooring here. I'm all for hardwood, and I love parquet: new or reclaimed, in any pattern. Floor tiling usually underlines hallways and high-traffic areas, but it still thrills me in a living room. Fun fact, vintage floor tiles generally run thicker than modern ones. Stone or Travertine tiles look breathtaking, but you'll need lots of supersoft area rugs if you want to live in a stone living space.

As with every other aspect of home design, trends come and go. As much as I would encourage you to go bold, pause before you pursue a totally brand-new flooring concept. Repainting a wall is one thing; ripping out and reinstalling flooring is a whole other ball game. Synthetic or vinyl plank flooring is delightfully affordable and easy to install, and with natural-looking textures and tones, it looks great. But it might not weather as well as more expensive natural solutions, which have their own needs in terms of upkeep. Combinations of both, such as wood veneers on a plywood base, could provide the best of both worlds.

Zoning with Rugs

Area rugs can bring a room together, adding comfort and style, especially when layered with smaller rugs on top. Options run the gamut from flat or low pile weaves with a smaller rug pad underneath—trust me, transformative—through plush or shag rugs, to vintage boucherouite rag rugs from Morocco. For me, each piece should feel laid back and comfortable, but still have that luxe edge. **Make the look your own by keeping an eye out for special details such as hand tufting or natural fibers.**

Select an area rug smaller than the room but slightly larger than the area to cover. In the living space, it should fit underneath your sofa and armchairs or, at the very least, each piece's front legs, and it should lie a foot or two away from any walls. In an open-plan home, this approach will unify your living space or delineate separate zones. This strategy works especially well for small studio apartments. Use a small area rug to define the entryway, a larger one for the living space, another one for the sleeping area, and so on.

Warm-toned stone adds a little laid-back luxe.

Bright bold art
looks amazing in
calm color schemes.
Pick a contrast
color or go
totally tonal like
this muted wool
masterpiece.

STORAGE SOLUTIONS

Every room should contain at least several books, but bookshelves, whether built in or installed smartly to fit the space well, can hold and display lots of other items that you want to showcase, such as family photos or heirlooms; a personal collection of small objects; vases or other small sculptural pieces; candles not in use; and so on.

For items that you don't want to display—pillows, blankcts, bolsters, board games, coasters, magazines, seasonal decorations, remote controls, charging cables, and more—**you have as many options as the size of the space will allow**. Placed behind a sofa, a credenza creates a structural grouping and gives you lots of handy storage space. A coffee table with multiple levels or drawers also makes good sense, as do enclosed end tables and even an ottoman with a built-in storage compartment.

ACCESSORIES

Keeping Your Space Fresh and Inviting

Every room needs fresh flowers, and you can buy them affordably at most grocery stores, box stores, and even warehouse stores. For the living room, create simple arrangements in vases that align with your decor. At thrift stores and yard sales, **you can find vases for practically pennies**; no need to spend a fortune on this small element that still has tremendous payoff.

PARTNERS IN CRIME

Choosing the Perfect Interior Designer

If you're hiring help, you need to ask questions and take a close look at the portfolio and personal style of the people whom you're considering. When I was in my 20s, my mother and I went to a fabric store to buy drapery fabric for her dining room. A woman in the shop started talking with my mother, and it turned out that she worked as an interior decorator. She pitched her services, but the way she dressed—quirky, very colorful, bold—didn't come remotely close to my mom's simple, classic style. *Why in the world would Mom hire you to design for her?* I thought. One designer may do a superlative job with organization and storage, but she may not match your aesthetic or understand how you want your home to feel. On the flip side, you may find someone with exactly your sense of style, but he may not fit your spatial planning needs.

Did someone say "perfect interior designer"? You know where to find me!

The Designer Drill

Questions to Ask a Potential Designer

Before committing money and time to a design professional, here's what you need to know.

1. **Can you work within the aesthetic I've identified?**
   Before an initial meeting, pin or mood board as many images as possible that represent the look that you want. The more images, the better to determine a good fit. My aesthetic runs fairly broad, but I probably couldn't do some looks as well as others. Those muted, quietly folksy, gallery-like interiors just aren't me.

2. **How do you know whether this project will work for you or your company? What about it interests you?**
   This question sounds like a job-interview question because it is. You literally are interviewing someone for a job! The answer should reveal how the designer thinks about design and, of course, what attracts him or her to your project—aside from the money. Maybe it's the challenge of your budget or the quirky features of your house. You may be offering an opportunity to embrace new technology or materials, extra important for the kitchen (page 117). If you agree with the answer, that's a good sign.

3. **What tool(s) will you use to show me the plans for my project?**
   Clients often don't ask this question because they don't know that different options exist. Those full-color, computer-generated rooms that magically appear in real time on *Bargain Mansions* and other renovation shows can cost about $20,000. That's an entire kitchen budget for some people! When my design group does a rendering, it doesn't look as sophisticated as on television, but one of those renderings can cost between $1,000 and $2,000, whereas a floor plan might cost only $400. I'd rather put the financial difference between a rendering and a floor plan into the project itself, but some people need that extra level of visual detail to feel comfortable. Discussing options and prices with your designer ahead of time works a lot better than getting a bill for something that you didn't need or expect.

4. **Do you welcome my involvement, or do you prefer me to keep a distance?**
   Some designers like complete creative control. If you love that person's entire portfolio, you may be okay with staying away until the final reveal. If you quake at making decisions, it can be a blessing to work with someone who knows exactly what to choose for what you want to achieve. After agreeing on a plan, some designers don't like to consult with clients further. That may sound harsh, but even collaborative designers don't like big surprises, such as "Hey, my grandmother just died, and I want you to incorporate her Victorian oak sideboard into the reno of my midcentury kitchen, which I know is half done already." (It happens more often than you'd think, and it's the stuff of nightmares!) Some designers consult with clients about

> **It can be a blessing to work with someone who knows exactly what to choose for what you want to achieve.**

every single decision, which kills surprises along with efficiency. Most designers fall somewhere in the middle, but it's always best to find out how the person likes to work before finding out the hard way that it's not what you expected or wanted.

5. **What inspires you?**
   The answer to this question will help determine whether you share the same spirit of design. If a potential designer loves high-tech materials and sleek minimalist design but you're a crunchy nature girl, slam the brakes. Ask to see the person's favorite projects and explain why those projects hold such a special place in the portfolio. A good designer may ask about your favorite colors, foods, books, pastimes, or travel destinations. Don't be afraid to flip the question to see whether you share the same aesthetic.

6. **When you think about a mistake you've made, what was it, how did you handle it, and what did you learn?**
   Yes, this is another job-interview question. You're hiring a designer to avoid costly mistakes that you might make if you did the work yourself. But we all are human, and all designers have made mistakes or run into situations that resulted in broken promises. How someone explains what happened—with insults or blame versus a more even-keeled narrative—dealt with those challenges, and applied lessons learned to future projects will tell you a lot about the person's working character.

7. **When working with a modest or tight budget, how do you prioritize what to spend where?**
   Unlimited budgets are great, but most of us don't live in that world. This question goes to the heart of where a designer wants to spend your money and where you both can make concessions. You can't cut corners on infrastructure, such as electrical and plumbing, and you should run from anyone who suggests the possibility of doing that. But for the specific project, does the designer think the flooring is more important than the appliances? Can she achieve the same great look with a stock lighting fixture, sink, and faucet to put more money toward gorgeous countertops and showstopping tile? What about the finishes? Your values should align here so you don't face any surprises when the final bill comes due.

Home Stories

ARTIST'S RESIDENCE

This home once belonged to the owners' Portuguese grandparents. The grandmother, who they adored, had been an artist, and they wanted to restore the house to something that she would have appreciated. No pressure! Her art had a freeness and femininity to it that I wanted to reflect in the home. In this small living space, with multiple doors and direct access to the outside, the pale Carrara marble fireplace served as the obvious focal point. This iridescent mermaid-esque tile in a herringbone pattern felt like something that the grandmother would have chosen, and soft blue walls added to a luxe look.

Pro Tip

Learn a little about the history of your home and try to nod to it in your design choices—it works.

ST.TROPEZ SOLEIL

LIVING AT SCALE

This circular fireplace was 6 feet tall. I fit inside it! But it was tiled and, like the rest of the house, looked tired and overdecorated. For a single dad and his three young daughters, the home had a unique brief. It needed something dramatic, masculine, but also cozy. Tonal paintwork harmonized with the stonework to simplify the space while contrasting with bold black tones. Cladding the wall, the custom-cut, cold-rolled steel fire surround has a subtle iridescence. The addition of modern open shelving and slouchy dueling sofas supported family time. In the corner, huge, floor-length windows replaced a set of doors, making the space safer when the girls enjoy the backyard pool, and created a secondary reading area.

THE COCKTAIL ROOM

In this space for conversation, you might just sit, read, and have coffee; sip cocktails; or both. The beautiful dramatic chandelier, quirky blue design on the blinds, and the rug zoned it beautifully. On the back wall, two cabinets added symmetry, and I love the position of the four chairs around the blush pink ottoman atop the dark, Brazilian cherry floor. The only strong colors come from the blinds and pillows, yet it feels like an upbeat, vibrant space.

UPSCALE HANGOUT SPACE

On several acres of land, this open-plan house needed an impressive entertaining space. At their church, the owners lead big youth groups, and every week they host 20 to 30 young people. It's not a massive home, so the couple wanted better flow throughout. Removing a huge, black, wooden mantel gave the living space more room to breathe. Installing this layered stone fireplace and four chandeliers, whitewashing the walls, and lightening the beams—boxing them in white oak—refocused the whole room into a spacious, easy-to-use hangout space. (Disguised in the shiplap is a hidden door to the primary bedroom.)

THE BLUE ROOM

The family who lives here are all about *color.* They wanted a living space with big personality. This room already had great trim work, but it needed *more.* Blue gloss paintwork in a shade that feels both formal and more playful than you might expect kept the house's traditional vibe but took it up a notch. (Gloss paint has both beauty and function. With three young kids in this home, gloss proves wonderfully hard-wearing and easy to wipe clean.) For contrast, the sofas and fireplace have calmer, more natural tones, and gold-foiled wallpaper stretches across the entire ceiling.

MODERN VINTAGE MAKEOVER

A friend's family owns this early 1980s house, and he grew up in it, making the renovation a real labor of love. The space had seen better days, and the project had its challenges—black widow spiders and *lots* of cats—but it was fun to see it come together. In a rustic midcentury vibe, box beams draw attention to the high ceiling, and fantastic woodlike chandeliers added so much light. But the real drama comes from the black tile wall, drawing the eye through the room. Natural textures, including wood, leather, and fresh flowers, and natural shapes, including the log-holder and lights, soften the series of bold decisions and straight lines.

CHECKLIST

- ☐ Be honest with yourself about how and how often you might use this room and design with function and beauty in mind.
- ☐ Create multiple focal points with table lamps, sconces, and standing lamps.
- ☐ When planning your layout, think comfort, conversation, and secondary uses, such as working from home, eating, reading, kids' things, and cocktails.
- ☐ Narrow sofa styles to options that speak to you, then let your butt choose.
- ☐ Carefully plan artwork before hanging it.
- ☐ Use soft materials to transition the space from day to night.
- ☐ Perfectly place your TV or consider a screen-free space.
- ☐ Be honest with your budget and invest in everyday.
- ☐ Consider a bar cart or extra surfaces to style for visual interest.
- ☐ Embrace luxurious flooring and rugs that you love.
- ☐ Deploy storage strategically.
- ☐ Accessorize with fresh flowers and thrifted objects for a low-budget instant upgrade.
- ☐ Hire help and brief the perfect design partner.

4

DINING SPACES

HAVE A SEAT TO EAT

In new builds today, separate dining rooms have become more uncommon than in the past. These days, people favor a more open-plan lifestyle, merging dining areas with kitchens or family rooms for a bigger, brighter, airier way of living—and I love that. Because people love open spaces, separate dining rooms in older homes, like mine, are becoming increasingly underappreciated and underused.

In an ideal world, the footprint of *every* home would integrate the dining space into the kitchen. But that's not always feasible, and if your dining room is collecting dust, it's easy to bring it back to life by using it as intended or expanding its functionality.

Some food for thought. **Give occasional spaces *more* attention, not less.** Once you've addressed the room's function and made it comfortable, have some fun! Use that banana leaf wallpaper that you bought for a song, that thrifted pink vintage chandelier that looks like a Murano Tronchi lamp, that ceramic bust of Arnold Schwarzenegger in *Terminator*, or that oversize artwork that's been sitting in storage for too long. Go a little crazy!

A SEAT AT THE TABLE

Designing the Perfect Dining Space

If you have a dining room that needs to be a dining room, let's start there. It needs to function primarily as an entertaining space, so aim your upgrade toward that function: table, chairs, and surfaces for serving platters and glassware. Will the table sit in the center of the space? Will it extend? Will it have drawers for essentials? For a small apartment, what about a wall-mounted, fold-down table or bar stools at a counter? Do you have room for built-in seating, such as a luxurious banquette? Would a coffee area liven the space, or would you prefer a fridge full of beer or Champagne? Your answers to those questions will drive most of the design.

Happiest when your table is a riot of bright tones and tacos? Me too.

There's nothing so characterful as a sprawling wooden farmhouse table.

Essential Tip: All meals should include pasta, bread, and too much butter.

DECOR

Mixing Styles for Added Character

My designs use a combination of modern and vintage style, and the dining room is no exception. My vintage dining table and chairs once belonged to my in-laws. Re-covering the chairs gave them new life alongside a more modern buffet with a lot of dimension to it.

LIGHTING

Dropping It Low

As you know, a comprehensive lighting system will create intimate moments and zone the space. **Start with a series of low pendants as part of a bigger system** that might include table lamps for mood, sconces to draw the eye, and can lights for moments when you need extra brightness (cleaning up or assembling puzzles, perhaps). Your pendant should range between a soft glow and something stronger. Add a dimmer switch, if you can. You don't want to have to use your phone's flashlight to see what you're eating. (I've been that person because it eventually happens to us all!) A couple of can lights close to the pendant can work magic here, or a series of ultraslim, rechargeable table lamps that will glow all night. Sconces and picture lights add visual interest, especially when highlighting niches and nooks. Add candles to the mix, and you've created a truly layered lighting scheme.

Install your pendants within the measurements of your table to avoid head-bumps.

SERVING TRADITION

Eating with Friends and Family

Cooking for loved ones can mean throwing a themed dinner party, celebrating big holidays, or marking important milestones. Decorating for get-togethers, planning games, and thinking up cocktails (other than my go-to, the Bee's Knees: gin, honey syrup, lemon juice—yum) add to the fun. Done right, it fosters closeness and community and can lead to a regular event—even if that's just ordering pizza, lighting candles, and drinking some good wine. Even just pizza night can become more meaningful than you might think!

Pro Tip

Start a regular meal club and use your dining space for what it's designed for.

SPECIAL EVENTS

How to Dress Your Dining Space

Whoever came up with the word *tablescaping*, thank you! For years, color schemes, centerpieces, and floral arrangements beautified my dining table, so it's nice to see that other people also consider it an art. (I feel like I already have my tablescape accreditation!) Making dining tables look good takes planning and a lot of creativity. Billowing a full tablecloth for a simple meal feels like too much, but **for a special event, layer fabrics**.

Instead of a single tablecloth, use Belgian linen, slightly wrinkled and with raw-edged hems, plus a couple of runners in different directions. Placing an undercloth beneath a tablecloth embraces tradition, but you can make your tabletop as formal or as casual as you like.

Give guests about 2½ feet each. Large events and meals often require squishing in, but it's still good to know the ideal measurement.

Think about crockery and cutlery. Salad plates or bowls look great stacked on the main plate. Add glasses for red and white wine, water glasses, and pitchers of ice water infused with citrus, cucumber, or herbs.

Balance height and scale. Bud vases with spindly single stems—ranunculus, for example—look great, as does a showstopping floral or edible centerpiece . . . but not at the expense of conversation. Your guests shouldn't have to banter through vegetation. For oval or rectangular tables, create something long rather than high.

You can use cutlery as part of a tablescape. Among the centerpieces, **arrange silverware in a series of vessels** rather than around the plates. It's a great way to channel farmhouse wedding style and start conversations around the table.

TABLETOP ESSENTIALS

Tableware and Accessories for All Your Dining Adventures

1. Tapered candles in simple candlesticks always look great. No scented candles here. Let the food aromas take center stage.
2. Place fresh foliage and flowers in a variety of vessels: branches in giant pickle jars, flowers from your garden or the store in traditional vases, or (my favorite) single blooms in small bud vases.
3. A cake stand and glass cloche create height, add visual interest, and if you use my cookie jar trick (page 44), build anticipation. The combination instantly makes an attraction of whatever you put in it.
4. Your oven-to-table serving ware (that casserole pot and lasagna dish) and trivets should look presentation-worthy. Before you place the pots in the oven, quickly wipe the inner and outer edges to prevent baked-on marks.
5. A variety of well-considered glassware can look as formal, casual, or unusual as you like. Flip the script and go for rocks glasses for wine and stemmed glasses for water, if you want. Estate sales and flea markets offer so much glassware, sometimes for a dollar apiece. It's so easy to find something to suit your taste.
6. Don't forget little necessities. Add a small dish for olive stones, shrimp shells, or cocktail skewers. Sauces and mustards need little spoons. An extra set of salt and pepper shakers never hurts, and multiple servings of butter whisper "luxury." Vintage salt wells at place settings can double as tiny bud vases.
7. Puzzles and art materials for the young and the restless make for a more successful meal.

MAKING A MEAL OF IT

Simple Ways to Elevate Mealtimes

Unusual design choices in a room that is often separated or closed off from other spaces draw you in and make you want to use it, but your design considerations shouldn't stop there. These tabletop ideas for inside or outside meal times set the mood and get the conversation flowing.

↑ **Mix and match dishes to create eye-catching, colorful place setting compositions.**

←
Consider unconventional centerpieces. Skip the flowers here and try displays of fruit, figurines, candlesticks, or even memorabilia, such as small, framed photos.

↓ Go natural with fresh potted herbs, plants, or pine sprigs, or go festive by writing notes or fortunes and wrap them in dinner napkins for guests to find at New Year's celebrations.

→
Mix it up. Dining rooms can feel fresh and inviting with a blend of sleek, contemporary designs and fun details. Swap out your plates, napkins, or flatware to keep things interesting. Contrast a modern, minimalist plate or gold flatware with a cute napkin to keep things real and personal.

STORAGE SOLUTIONS

Keeping Your Dining Space Clutter-Free

After you reinvigorate your dining room, perhaps enhancing its multifunctionality, that perfectly clean and clear space can teeter on becoming the clutter room again. Having good storage here sets up the space for its many possible uses. (In my dining room cupboards, you'll find holiday crockery, kids' trinkets, puzzles, office files, and more.)

If you have the space, **built-in cupboards and open shelves balance functionality and beauty**, and a ready-to-go tray of everyday table essentials, such as silverware, napkins, placemats, and a salt and pepper set, acts as a go-bag for unexpected dining moments.

After you clear the table, dress it for non-eating occasions. A large, leafy fern, some coffee table books, or a fruit bowl could stop you from tossing delivery boxes on it as you pass through the space.

Combine open and closed shelving for a storage solution that's easy on the eye.

Smaller Spaces

No dining room? No problem. That low-hanging pendant light with its soft, downward beam can transform any location, even a kitchen counter, into an intimate or event-focused eating area. **Using a special table treatment further defines the space.** Woven rattan or scallop-edged linen placemats, vintage cloth napkins, an eye-catching salt and pepper set only for dinnertime, special water glasses—they all help make for memorable moments.

> "In my dining room cupboards, you'll find holiday crockery, kids' trinkets, puzzles, office files, and more."

Use It or Improve It

Quick Fixes for Alternate Uses

1. **Home Office:**
   Remove all your dining chairs except one, set up your computer, and video chat to your heart's content with your feet on the table (the biggest desk you've ever had) safely offscreen.
2. **Yoga Space:**
   A dedicated yoga or meditation space represents true laid-back luxe. This option works best if you can close your dining room door while doing downward dog.
3. **Kids' Playroom:**
   Start by letting the table become a craft zone. Add a combination of open shelves for storage bins, cupboards for storage bins, and baskets for storage bins. You can't have enough storage in a kids' playroom. Don't forget to add floor cushions and pillows in hard-wearing, outdoor fabrics.

Home Stories

ZONING WITH COLOR

I was on a tight budget when I designed this, but you really can't tell. It feels as dramatic and inviting as any other. At the edge of the kitchen, this once-overlooked, walk-through space incorporated an exterior door and seemed unusable. Adding top-to-bottom floating shelves and painting the wall black made a feature of dishware storage. Small, framed art pieces with large white borders provided contrast, and the pendant light zoned the area. This look easily could work in a small house or apartment.

A NOD TO TRADITION

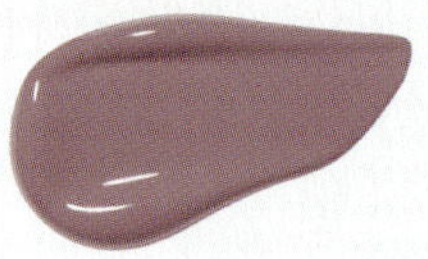

Paint color: Farrow and Ball Sulking Room Pink

The owner of this house grew up in it and purchased it from her parents. In the 1980s, her mother picked the floral wallpaper and covered every inch of the room, floor to ceiling, as was the style then. Beautiful in its day, but the current owner and her husband had grown tired of the design. It needed an upgrade, but I liked the paper, so I asked them to trust me. I installed trim work three-fourths of the way up the wall, painting it a beautiful dusty blue color-matched to the wallpaper with my Nix Mini gadget. Other additions included hardwood floors and a beautiful linear light fixture over the table. Refinishing her parents' table and chairs transformed them from dark mahogany to a paler, more contemporary shade. The remaining strip of wallpaper honored the history of the house—and the family.

Paint color: Benjamin Moore Brittany Blue

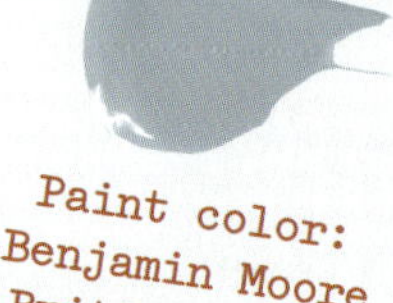

I wanted the perfect sconces so I designed my own! These are my Charlotte lights by Quorum.

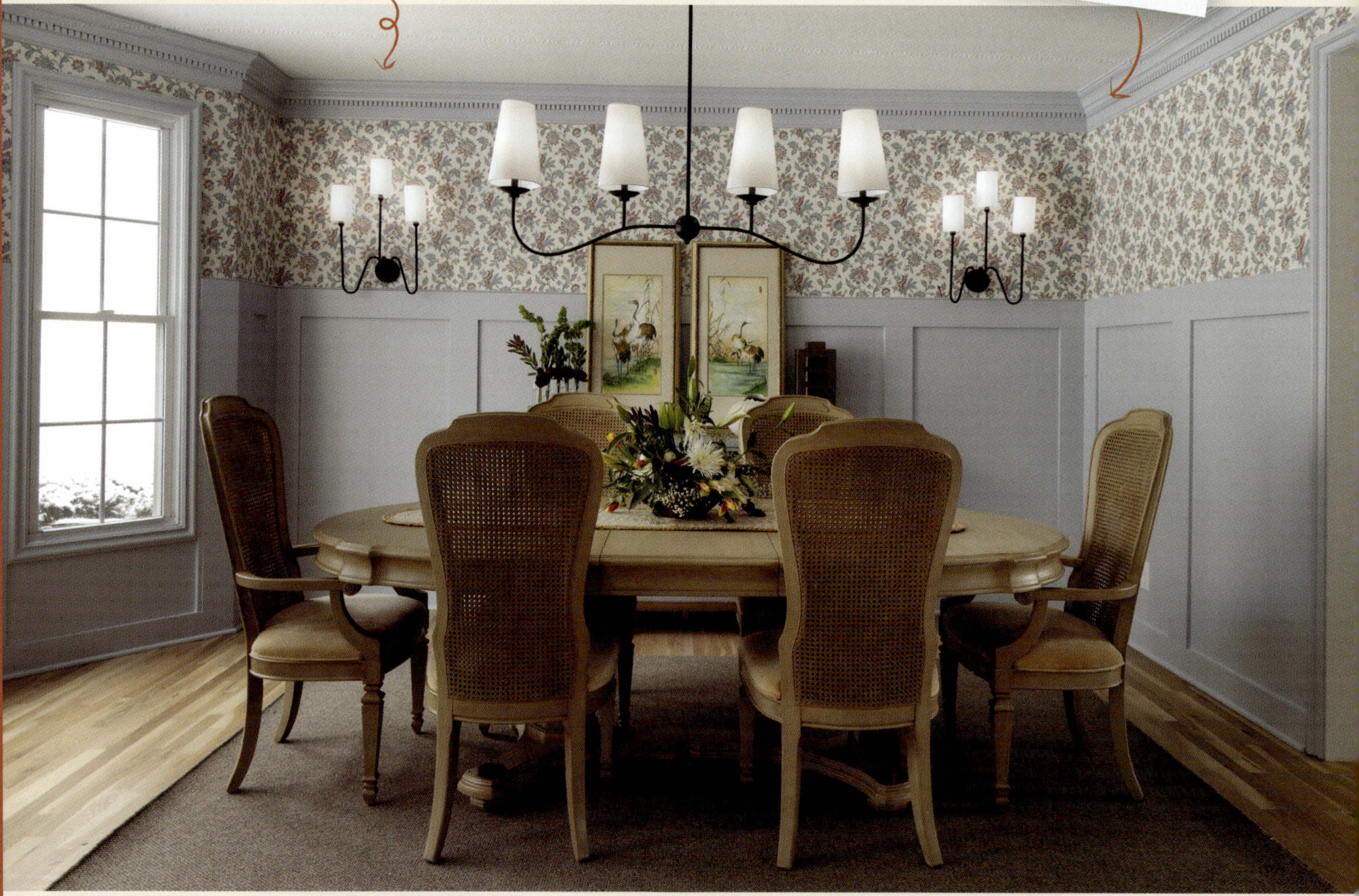

BOTANICAL VINTAGE

This delightful client said that she wanted to play it safe, but her favorite references looked bold and interesting. A good designer understands a client's visual vocabulary and what someone is saying even when not saying it. So this room evolved from its 1980s burgundy palette and went all out with dusty rose paintwork, trim in a special plaid formation, a statement set of palm-leaf pendants, and a bold print wallpaper. The client's husband had said "just no flowers," so let's call it botanical (wink). In the end, the bold new room worked, and the client loved it.

I took a risk with this room and it paid off. It's good to be bold sometimes!

DINING IN SMALL SPACES

This delightful dining space in an eat-in kitchen needed to become family friendly. The homeowners had small children, so it had to be easy to clean and look interesting. The answer? Tiling the entire area, floor to ceiling. The tiles came in geometric sheets, and the raw edge looked so good that it worked as a feature without the usual trim. **Custom banquettes work great for awkward corners, provide tons of storage space, and save on space** because you need at least 2 feet of floor space per dining chair. An odd number of industrial-style statement pendants at different lengths added a fun, playful feel that didn't feel too fussy. Pillows and a fabric remnant in Belgian linen as a runner softened the space.

Tonal grouting on this stone-clad wall adds a muted vibe.

BANQUETTE OF DREAMS

This house belongs to one of my crew, a world-class tile setter, and it was a pleasure to work on his home. Working well together made it even more fun to make dramatic updates, including the stone cladding, built-up wood stove hood, and—rather than an eat-at kitchen island—a custom banquette upholstered in an abstract art piece that my friend Kelly O'Neil made and printed on fabric. Note the ogee edge of what otherwise would be a waterfall island rendered in marble. **Waterfall edges remain a strong contemporary trend, but a decorative ogee edge or thick, substantial-looking mitered edge looks timeless.**

For a banquette, the seat should tilt back a little for back support.

GRAPHIC AND BOLD

This open-plan modern mid-century home needed a zoned-off dining area achieved with this luxe rug. To reflect the existing tones of black, white, and gray elsewhere in the home, this perfect geometric encaustic-like glass tile created an upscale look. Tiling a whole wall, from ceiling to floor, delineated the dining space. That's gold glitter grout. Yep, you can glam midcentury! Brass-toned open shelving and cantilever chairs added warmth, while the retro crystal chandelier with chrome detail added extra luxe. **You don't always have to match all your metals. Sometimes, it looks better if you freestyle it.**

FORMAL AND FABULOUS

In this modern Tudor-style home, a simple design embraced the family's roots and love of Asian history and culture. The brief called for evoking their travels and childhood memories, but with formality. The room itself stayed simple and elegant, with the addition of mural wallpaper: a mountainscape with dove grays and pinks and a tree shaped like a Japanese maple. The soft blush walls harmonize with the wallpaper, and star-shaped light fixtures with handcrafted wood beads add a traditional, craft feel. **Murals look fantastic on walls that don't have a lot of furniture interfering with the design**, so this space offered a perfect mural moment. It's still the most formal dining room I've ever created, and I completely love it.

CHECKLIST

- ☐ Make this space work for what you already do. Start with function, end with delight.
- ☐ Create an atmospheric, useful lighting system: bright enough to eat without needing a flashlight.
- ☐ Mix decor styles and incorporate heirlooms and hand-me-downs, revitalizing them with new upholstery, new colors, or hardware.
- ☐ Create new traditions: pizza night, board game night, Friday night cocktails and snacks.
- ☐ Elevate mealtimes with thoughtful, fun tablescapes, thrifted finds, layered fabrics, surprising centerpieces, even unexpected items on a cake stand.
- ☐ Consider those often-forgotten details: your oven-to-table dishes, trivets, salt cellars, and bud vases.
- ☐ Use storage to tidy the space for daytime uses.
- ☐ No dining room, no problem. Use lighting and table treatments to define the eating area.
- ☐ Use it or improve it: Challenge yourself to do something *in* this space and *with* this space, from home office to yoga studio.

5 KITCHENS

SOMETHING'S COOKING

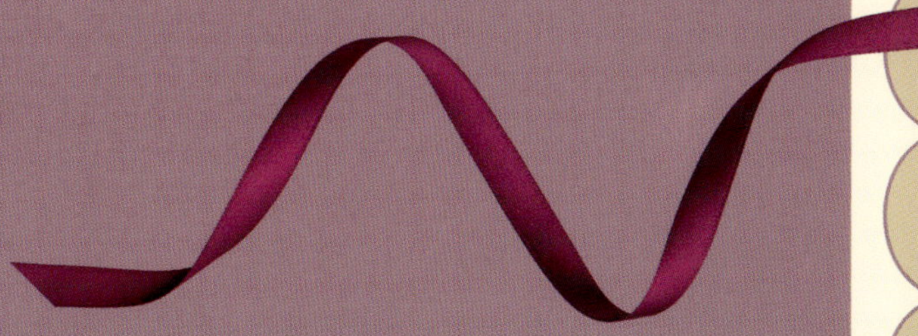

WHAT'S COOKING, GOOD LOOKING?

When I was a kid, my family moved around so much that sometimes my mom's delicious cooking felt like the only constant: mulberry cherry pie, pillowy soft pumpkin rolls, chicken with homemade noodles and gravy that I now make for my own family. She showed me how the kitchen can represent the heart of a home. My grandparents' busy farm kitchen functioned not only as a working space but also a place of fun and discovery. It kept the house running with endless meals, moonlighting as an office and lab for Grandpa's farm work, while serving as a warm, inviting space for baking, gossip, and the occasional prank (a joke-store firework in Grandpa's end-of-day cigarette). "I knew Tamara was in town if there was a finger swipe through the frosting," my grandmother said, and not much has changed. Baking makes me happy, and I can't keep my fingers out of the frosting bowl.

When I design a new kitchen for clients, those summers and their unique combination of work and pleasure come back to me. The space inspired us all. Mom and Grandma tried new recipes, passing their knowledge to us kids, and Grandpa farmed wheat. After dinner, at golden hour, we walked the fields. Through patience and perseverance, he created a new variety, the number one cultivar grown in Kansas for decades. (He named it Tut wheat, after the Treasures of Tutankhamun exhibition that toured America in the late 1970s and made everyone Tut-crazy.) He had his best ideas in the kitchen. Those summers and that kidlike sense of excitement and creativity continue inspiring my design aesthetic today.

More than any other space in the home, your kitchen needs to work for you. With my tips, tricks, and suggestions, you can make anything look pretty (*anything*), but an awkward layout, clunky cabinetry, too long of a path between ice machine and a place to sit, or nowhere to put your favorite dishes, and you'll hit the boiling point. But here's the good news. From the teeniest rental kitchenette, through renovating the kitchen you have now, to designing and building something grand and brand-new, you have opportunities for beauty and function everywhere.

FOOD
MARTHA STEWART'S
HANDMADE HOLIDAY CRAFTS
KitchenAid

Everyone wants something better: more space, more impact, better design. People often have strong ideas of color and style, a content creator whose work they love, design elements that they've craved for years, or a beloved piece of furniture or art to incorporate. Sometimes, clients ask me to work from scratch, drawing on my knowledge of what's new in the appliance, fixture, and lighting markets; my experience; and my hands-on approach. (If you've seen *Bargain Mansions*, you know how I go wild with a sledgehammer!)

The main reason for renovating and reconfiguring a kitchen space is that it isn't working. Does any of this sound familiar? There's nowhere to put down hot dishes or unpack groceries. A lack of cabinet and cupboard space means unpacking and repacking them to find that little gadget that always hides in the back. The fridge is too small, or it has the freezer section on top so you constantly have to bend down to reach for water and other everyday items. You love great coffee, but every time, you need to drag out the machine, reach around other stuff to plug it in, and stand there in your undies and bare feet at seven a.m. while it brews. You always bang your hip against that counter corner. The sink area looks too dark, the basin is too low, and your back hurts. The lights shine too bright. *It's just not working.*

You can make any kitchen look great with custom paint colors on the cabinets, vintage hardware, imported tiles, a quartz counter, thoughtful wainscoting, and original artwork. But if you can't cook in it, you can't live in it. A kitchen should express your style and look nothing short of amazing, but practicality needs to underpin everything.

A dream kitchen actively considers the people working in it. Its layout should make life easier, not harder. A functional, good-looking space can encourage togetherness for loved ones who, let's face it, usually gravitate here. It can inspire home cooking or, if you don't cook, make you feel like you want to try. It even can work as an entertaining space for a cocktail or two.

So let's get cookin'!

If you follow one rule, it should be this: Make your kitchen a space you actually want to spend time in.

WHERE TO BEGIN

First Things First

Start with your childhood kitchen, a friend's home you love, a vacation rental that over-delivered, or even a hotel suite that you didn't want to leave. Identify what you liked about the style, storage, and organization of each space. Seriously, make a list! To help do that, ask yourself these questions that I ask my clients.

- Was everything within reach? Was the path among sink, stove, and refrigerator clear and easy to navigate?
- Was the space easy to keep clean?
- What worked well, and what didn't?
- Did the appliances overwhelm the space, or were they hidden cleverly from view?
- Was the fridge too small or too big?
- If a window sat above the sink, did you like that, or did you not like having to turn away from the rest of the kitchen to use it?

Now, think about your existing kitchen. What do you like, and what drives you crazy?

- Does it have enough properly configured storage? Is everything hidden neatly away, or would you rather have your frequent and favorite items on view?
- Are you missing seating for quick, thrown-together meals? Do you need an area for admin or homework?
- If you have kids interested in cooking or baking, what might help them learn and achieve eventual independence in the kitchen?
- How does the whole household use the space? Has your family grown, or have their needs changed? Does your dog need a hangout area in here?
- Wait, do you need a wine fridge? (Trick question; the answer is yes!)

Pro Tip

Hone in on the world around you—your favorite coffee shop or restaurant, perhaps, or your best friend's home—wherever you find design you admire. Sketch it out, note it down, and use it as a starting point.

LAYOUT

Planning the Perfect Kitchen

For redesigning and renovating older homes, open the kitchen as much as possible. When built, the once-grand, now antique mansions of Kansas City didn't use the kitchen as the hub of the house. At the back of the house, cooking staff worked in small spaces by modern standards. Meals took place in the formal dining room (page 91), more of a bygone practice today. By increasing the space and installing luxe countertops and painted cabinetry or modern open shelves, you can keep a harmonious blend of old and new.

Planning begins with imagination, but plumbing or gas lines might limit installation options. That old 1940s idea of the kitchen work triangle—keeping a tight, efficient path among sink, stove, and refrigerator—matters more in smaller, traditional kitchen spaces, but having everything within easy reach still matters in bigger kitchens, too. You don't want to have to walk the long way around a huge island every time you need butter from the fridge. (Julia Child was right: "With enough butter, anything is good.")

Case in point. A client was building his dream home with the help of a genius architect. The location and plans looked breathtaking, seriously one of the most gorgeous projects ever. But it had a layout problem. The route from garage to kitchen stretched *waaay* too long. **Keep the path to unpack groceries or take out the trash as simple, clear, and short as possible.** Otherwise, it'll feel like training for a marathon, and the kitchen isn't the place for that. Luckily, the client was able to tweak the floor plan before work started. From rental studio to brand-new mansion, the same principle applies. The kitchen layout needs to work for you.

Naturally cool stone countertops are perfect for making pastry and pasta.

This is my kitchen, full of must-haves and compromises, and I love it.

CHOOSING AN ISLAND

Living That Island Life

To island or not to island? That's the question. **A kitchen island makes great sense in airy, spacious homes, focusing all the action into one point.** The standard version consists of a single-slab counter—marble, quartz, quartzite, or stone—with cabinets and appliances underneath (perhaps in a color or material that contrasts with the cabinets), and maybe a sink, range, or both. **If you like to be social as you cook or want a more informal eating spot, add an overhang to create a sitting counter.** A waterfall edge—where the countertop continues down the sides and meets the floor—gives a dramatic, on-trend look but isn't always the answer. For extra surface and storage, smaller spaces benefit from a movable island, such as an old butcher's block or kitchen cart, and they look adorable, too. My own kitchen island was a happy accident, but more on that later.

This pull-out wooden tabletop gives extra functionality for surprise dinner or cocktail guests.

CABINETS

Keep It Open, Closed, or Both

Kitchens that will see lots of sautéing and frying will benefit from closed cabinetry closest to the stove, but open shelving can work everywhere else, making space for kitchen gadgets that you use frequently or that you use occasionally but like seeing or still want at arm's reach. Plan for an electrician to install extra outlets (out of sight, on counter sides, under wall cabinets, even inside your pantry), which will make using your retro stand mixer or pasta-roller a dream.

Open shelving means more dusting, but that's a small price to pay for more space in one of the most important rooms in the home. **Adding accordion doors to open shelving gives you the option of both looks: open and eye-catching or clean and sleek**. Remember, it's not just about cabinets. Think about drawers, too. Do you prefer pull-out storage to static shelves? My kitchen has two generous refrigerator drawers cleverly disguised as cabinets, and who doesn't love pull-outs for the garbage and recycling?

Sanding, priming, and painting existing cabinets will save money and create a bespoke look, but if your kitchen needs brand-new cabinetry, invest in quality. You'll never regret it, especially because you can update the color and hardware in a jiffy to transform the look of your kitchen over a weekend. **Other low-effort updates to existing cabinetry include creating a contrast interior**—black for white cabinets, dark gray for light gray, ochre or goldenrod for navy blue, dusty rose for soft green—**adding new pull-out inserts, or installing glass shelves**.

Natural wood cabinetry with lots of visual texture always lends a warm, cozy vibe, even in an otherwise modern design.

KNOWING YOUR STYLE

Getting in Touch with Your Personal Style

Remember my handy-dandy checklist, "How to Style Any Room" (page 73)? If not, flip back to familiarize yourself with my field-tested formula, which works for any style. If you skipped to this chapter before reading the Entryways chapter (no judgment!), flip back to What's Your Style? (page 34) to find that out, too.

When we meet, my clients tell me about themselves, their daily lives, and how they live in each space. For the kitchen, they show me how they use theirs, telling me their dream dinner and how they'd make it. That information reveals what they need, what can work as a delightful, in-budget treat, and what will bring them joy. A huge part of a good relationship with clients entails uncovering their personal style, bringing clarity to their vision, and making them feel confident about it.

Clients often tell me that they love a particular kitchen from *Bargain Mansions*, but their mood-board references from magazines or online don't match my work on the show. Those references usually consist of white or light-wood spaces that feel plain, utilitarian, and lacking personality. That disconnect tells me that they're afraid of getting it wrong. My job starts with helping people identify and feel comfortable with their own style, what they *really* want.

MOOD BOARDS

Field Test Your Ideas

Build your own inspiration boards with paint, tile and countertop samples, dream hardware, fabric swatches, and photos.

Let your mood boards inspire a bespoke paint color—from warm wood to coffee grounds.

Pro Tip

Digital inspiration boards are great, but getting real samples in your hands—feeling their textures and seeing how they look in natural light—is always a winner.

My Unexpected Centerpiece

The centerpiece of my kitchen—a beautifully bashed-up wooden counter salvaged from a hardware store—offers a master class in creative compromise. The plan for my own renovation called for a perfect bespoke island, functional and beautiful, housing all my appliances, outlets, *and* the kitchen sink. (It still haunts my dreams!) But with the Great Recession, we had to manage our expectations, cut the budget, and change course. Something had to give. My original design went into a drawer, and I started estate sale-ing for something else to fill the space.

My eyes lit up as soon as they landed on it: an old wooden store counter that had aged naturally into a warm, honeyed tone. It needed some love—removing paint splatters, cleaning, and oiling—but it cost only $400. In the corner, cutting a small circle with a drawer underneath helped with catching crumbs and cleaning. (A salt dish now sits snugly in that hole.) An electrician wired the counter for me so I can plug everything that I need into it. Hardware from a Ralph Lauren counter salvaged from an old Dillard's department store, a beer bottle opener, and hooks dressed it up nicely. But you still can see traces of its past life. On a low shelf, out of view, runs a series of small black marks. The store clerk set his cigarette here, leaving tiny burn marks along that edge. They must have been really busy!

If your budget changes—which happens more than any of us would like—you'll have to rethink your original plan, which, I promise, isn't the end of the world. Keep an open mind, push your creativity, and drum up the confidence to do something different or unique. Is my kitchen island 100 percent perfect? Not quite. Do I completely love it? Absolutely.

COUNTERS

Embracing Counter Culture

Here are the usual suspects.

Granite

Classic, tough-wearing, and attractive, granite has lots of natural movement in its veining that works well for messier households.

Marble

It always looks incredible, but marble proves hard to keep clean. Maintaining the shine takes effort, and it stains easily. Consider marble trim or a single row of marble tiling along the backsplash for the vibe without the expense or hassle.

Quartz and Quartzite

In the kitchen, engineered quartz, meaning man-made and supertough, can withstand almost anything. Quartzite looks and costs more, like marble. Using slabs from the same block adds movement and drama throughout the space.

Tile

On a counter, white or pale grout stains easily, but good tiling looks, well, *good*. Cover the entire countertop or just certain areas, around the stove, for instance, or in a pantry. Tile countertops look very 1980s, but they totally are making a comeback.

Wood

Classic butcher-block countertops give a lively, warm vibe, but they need regular oiling and develop a used, well-loved look over the years, no matter how careful you are.

Dark, richly stained wood flooring helps balance pale-toned walls.

HARDWARE

Fixtures and Fittings to Transform Your Kitchen

The right handles and knobs, vintage or otherwise, can lift the look of cabinetry, giving it a more upscale feel. Hardware also has a practical element. Stone countertops work great for making pasta and pastry. One-piece backsplashes—rather than tiny, hard-to-clean tiles and grouting—can help messy chefs who always splatter sauce. For everyday cupboards, drawers, and appliances, **make sure your hardware feels comfortable to the touch and looks great**.

Paint color: Benjamin Moore Brittany Blue

Short of time and budget? Upgrading your hardware always has an outsized effect.

FLOORING

What Lies Beneath

At the end of the intro, you saw that we're gonna break some rules, right? Well, buckle up. **In the kitchen, wooden floors with the right finish work great**. If you already have a wooden floor in your kitchen, lightly sand it to smooth it out. Lighten it with a clear or slightly tinted varnish, stain it dark for a dramatic effect, or split the difference with an eye-catching checkerboard effect. Alternatively, have a flooring company install unfinished hardwood that you can finish yourself. If both of those options sound like too much work, invest in finished flooring ready to go the moment it's laid and locked into place.

Safely secured rugs and mats look great in this space, too. Wherever you do most of your standing, consider placing a squishy, antifatigue mat that matches the kitchen vibe.

Pro Tip

Hand-painted checkerboard floors are easy to install and age beautifully. Measure up, create a simple grid with painter's tape, and remove it before your floor paint is completely dry for the sharpest results.

LIGHTING

Layered Lighting for Function and Atmosphere

If you're reading this book front to back, you already know where this is going. The different pieces of layered lighting work together to create a welcoming, attractive environment neither too bright nor too dark. In kitchen design, functionality and versatility rule. But cleaning requires a brightness that would harsh any social gathering, and your prep area needs good lighting somewhere between those extremes. So install lighting from multiple sources. **Use pendants to mark an eating area or to make the island the room's focal point.** In nooks and walk-ins, small sconces or table lamps add dimension and warmth.

I love these bold, pine tree–inspired chandeliers.

STORAGE SOLUTIONS

Overthink This Kitchen Essential

For a home cook, nothing delights more than well-thought-out storage. But how much is too much? Great storage offers the perfect solution for creating a functional, striking kitchen.

Start by thinking about what kind of storage works best for you. Where are you lacking? Do you like everything packed away neatly, or do you prefer open shelves—or is there room for both? Are you unpacking rarely used holiday dishes just to access daily-use items or clattering noisily through saucepans and skillets every time you cook? Are you bending down too much, or reaching for a step stool all the time? Consider all possibilities to make your space accessible and extremely easy to use. You can't overthink this aspect of your kitchen.

Sometimes, you can add storage in the most unexpected places. In my own kitchen, the panels above the range hood were stationary, as in most cases because they're unreachable for most people. Behind each panel lies empty space. *Not on my watch!* I thought. Opening them and adding hinges created instant extra storage. All my holiday dishes live up there now. They come down to play only a couple of times a year and otherwise snooze safely there, stored away.

Pro Tip

For open shelving: If you have clear glasses and mugs and flatware in a single color, it won't matter much if they go back a little haphazardly because you already have nailed the aesthetic.

HITTING A SNAG

Changing the Unchangeable

Creating the perfect kitchen means visualizing, planning, and leaving as little to chance as possible. But learn from me and approach each project with the wisdom and patience that come from adjusting expectations, compromise, and going with the flow. **If you can't remove it, work with it or hide it.** In the immortal words of Sandra Lee Harris, a 1970s computer programmer, "It's not a bug, it's a feature."

In one kitchen that I renovated, an essential I-beam cut through the space and ruined my plans . . . until it occurred to me to box it in with faux cabinet doors. In another house, an ugly ventilation vent cut straight through the upper mezzanine level. As much as I wanted to remove it, it had to stay put, so we clad the vent shaft with bespoke shelving. The result looked gorgeous and unexpected, bringing an unplanned sense of fun and wonder to the space. Who doesn't want that?

The same principle applies small scale, too. Hide the thermostat behind a small, framed piece of artwork. Camouflage that ugly Wi-Fi router behind a thrift store find. You get the idea.

DESIGNING FOR YOURSELF

A Kitchen Just for You

Creating your dream home often means creating a discrete location for a favorite hobby: a crafting space, a sewing room, a painting studio, even what I call a Lego atelier—because why not? One of my *Bargain Mansions* clients, a fabulous woman, wanted a special area for a surprising kitchen hobby: canning. She *loves* preserving fruit and vegetables, so she requested a canning station. She wanted not only a comfortable, practical area to excel at her craft, but also a gallery to showcase all those gorgeous glass jars of peaches and okra. "I do it all the time. I need a special area," she said, and that's what she got! She knew herself so well and had such clarity of vision that it was a joy to work with her. Her canning salon looks wonderful, even if I say so myself.

Show off your goods with pocket-door cabinetry.

Home Stories

STORAGE TWO WAYS

Can't decide on open or closed shelving? Do both! Here, my client wanted storage that gave easy access to everything but felt ordered, calm, and minimal. A series of accordion doors achieved that goal, but as you can tell, I'm a maximalist at heart, so the story didn't end there. Each cupboard needed to have its "moment" so that, when opened, it revealed a fun and interesting pop of color. Each simple storage area became an inviting and intentional space, one for breakfast items, one for baking, and so on. A grid of mustard-gray tiles went in the back, with the whole thing set on the luxe stone countertop.

COLOR YOUR KITCHEN

This small kitchen of a guest suite/vacation rental formed part of a larger project. The homeowners live next door and wanted to achieve a *lot* in this space. My job consisted of creating a fun, memorable kitchen that looked just as inviting online as IRL. A pink ceiling with blush walls packed it full of visual interest. **For functionality, running open shelving across the window added extra storage without losing any light.** The shelves in the nook? That's a Murphy door that opens into the main house for easy access between spaces.

Paint color: Benjamin Moore Barberry

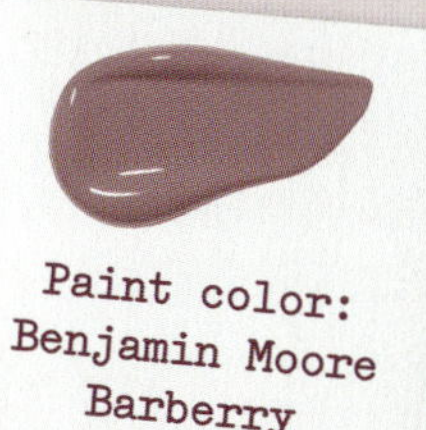

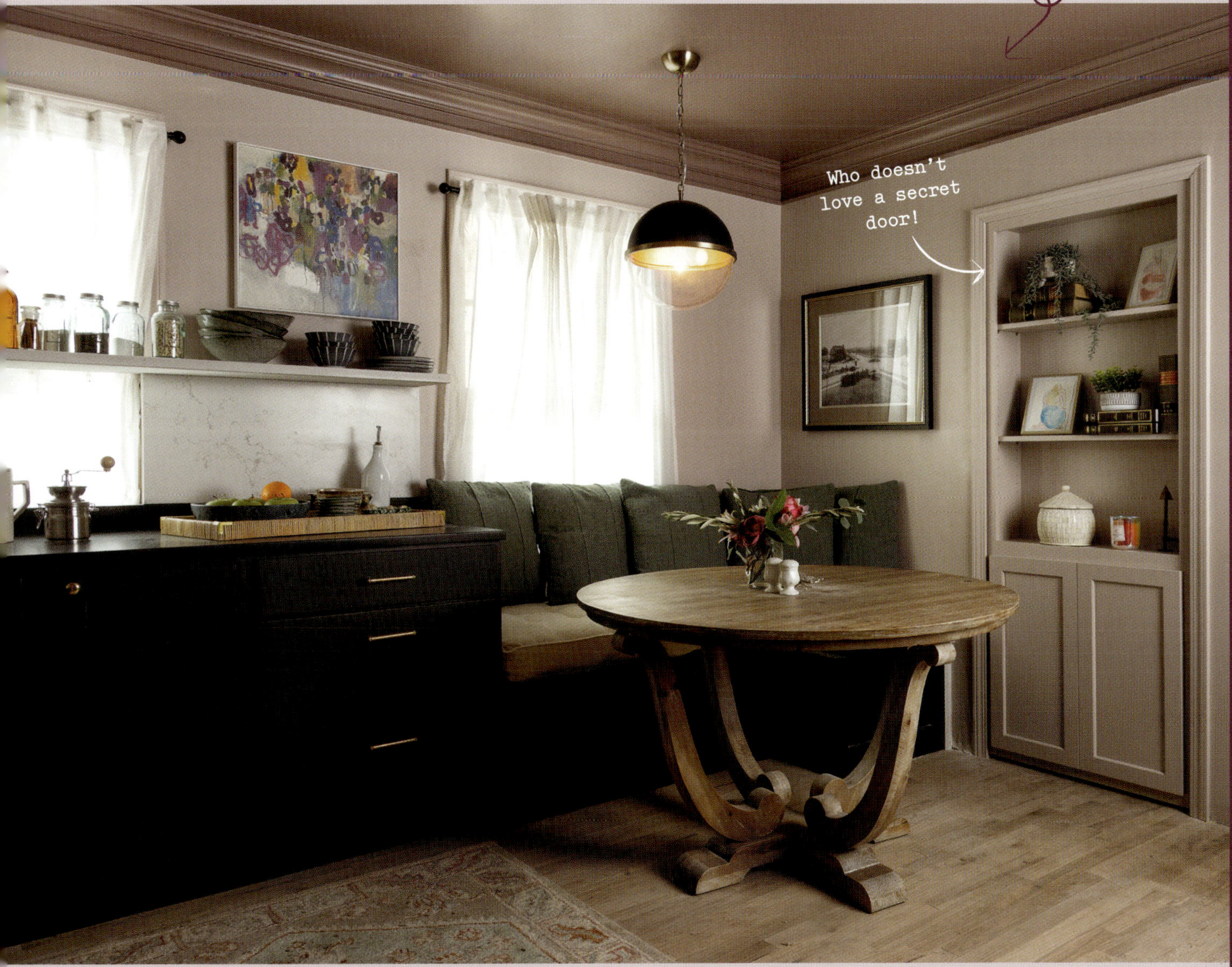
Who doesn't love a secret door!

THE SWINGING COUNTERTOP

In a rich, dramatic wood, this counter swings into different positions via a pivot system. The homeowners love to entertain and have a gorgeous deck, just out of view. Turned toward the stove, the counter can transform from an informal, eat-in area to a buffet surface. Swung the other direction and set with dishes, it directs traffic to the eating area overlooking a beautiful pond in the back. A pass-through window made outdoor eating even easier. **You'll never regret adding multifunctional, do-anything elements to your kitchen.**

Use wood from the same block to create a continuing visual interest.

BESPOKE TOUCHES

This might qualify as my favorite kitchen *of all time*. My clients had lived in the house for more than a decade and asked contractor after contractor to open their cramped kitchen space. No one suggested moving the entire room into a rarely used secondary living space next door—until I came along! Without hesitation, the couple agreed. (Love that!) The stunning new space features a vaulted ceiling, no upper cabinets, mink-brown paintwork, custom walnut side panels, and a huge island with gold inlay and custom brass feet. Best of all, the new walk-in pantry, with stunning marble and granite flooring, has more storage than in all of the previous kitchen.

A little goes a long way with custom-made detailing.

SCALE AND DRAMA

At 16 feet, this gorgeous dark wood, stone-capped kitchen island with seating and open shelving ranks among the longest that I've designed, but other elements make it noteworthy, too, including that it's wheelchair accessible. The two wooden cabinets hide a fully integrated refrigerator on one side and a walk-in pantry on the other. The bar features custom cabinetry, and an antique mirror echoes a window on the opposite side of the space. The ceiling height proved challenging, though. For such a wide space, it stood only 8 feet tall and felt too flat. The solution came in the form of faux box-trim design: a grid of one-by-four planks, with trim pieces left and right, a brass-toned custom hood above the stove, and a pot-filler faucet for a touch of drama.

CUSTOM-MADE ISLAND

Originally, this space looked totally Tuscan, full of swirling, scrolled details, dishes, and knickknacks, which the owners wanted to change. Installing a seamless, waterfall-style island here would have timestamped the space, which instead called for a more classical vibe that wouldn't date. Lombardi marble looks gorgeous but costs a lot, so thankfully the budget allowed for enough material to carry the veins down the sides. Adding a lip, called an ogee edge, around the top and custom marble baseboards helped attain that timeless feel. **Apron-front sinks sit an inch lower than the countertop, not great for your back, and they tend to splash. But an undermount sink with an apronlike strip of marble can achieve the same look.** Simplifying everything worked, as did adding a pantry full of display opportunities so those cherished tchotchkes still have pride of place.

Lively pale marble always looks great with warm metallic tones.

SECOND TIME'S THE CHARM

The homeowners loved this house so much that they bought it twice. The first purchase happened decades ago. A job transfer prompted them to sell and move, but years later, they transferred back and waited to buy it again. Their original teeny kitchen looked colorful but didn't function well. The second time around, they wanted more space and functionality. They also were willing to go bold, which they told me right out the gate. After I pitched a purple kitchen, the wife kicked the husband under the table and said, "We're going to do what Tamara says." He was sweating, I'm sure, but in the end, he agreed. Gold hardware, sconces, and pendants; Carrara marble counters and wainscoting, and an island on a checkerboard marble floor gave the kitchen a European formality that they and I love.

I just love bold cabinetry; it never disappoints.

Paint color: Sherwin Williams Merlot

ARCHWAY TO HEAVEN

Doorways are often an opportunity for a little considered design, and archways are one of my favorite features to install. The shape evokes classic architecture and, with the addition of a glass-paned pocket door, they're practical, too. In this home transformation, I used both to separate the kitchen from the laundry room and garage entrance. Open, it draws the eye and gives an airy feel, but closed it blocks out noise from the washer and dryer. I used an upbeat botanical wallpaper in the laundry room, but tiled the back wall in a way that echoed the kitchen design and gave a sense of continuity. It's heaven!

RECIPE FOR A DREAM KITCHEN

From years of renovating, redesigning, and flipping, I've created or consulted on *hundreds* of kitchen spaces. Here's my checklist of essentials to consider, my recipe for a dream kitchen, if you will.

- ☐ Layout
- ☐ Style
- ☐ Cabinets
- ☐ Counters
- ☐ Flooring
- ☐ Hardware
- ☐ Lighting
- ☐ Storage
- ☐ Appliances

6 FAMILY ROOMS

ALL TOGETHER NOW

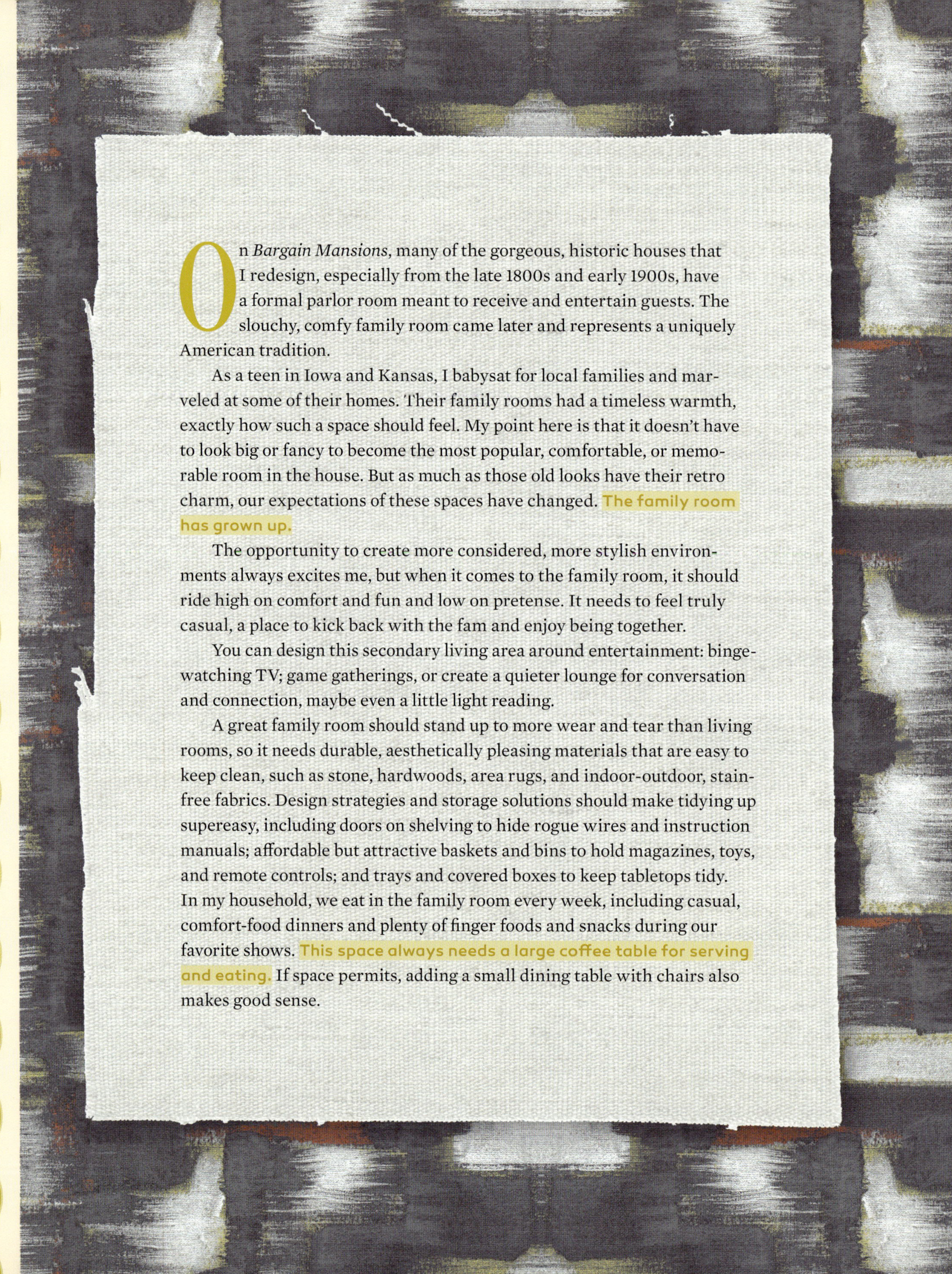

On *Bargain Mansions*, many of the gorgeous, historic houses that I redesign, especially from the late 1800s and early 1900s, have a formal parlor room meant to receive and entertain guests. The slouchy, comfy family room came later and represents a uniquely American tradition.

As a teen in Iowa and Kansas, I babysat for local families and marveled at some of their homes. Their family rooms had a timeless warmth, exactly how such a space should feel. My point here is that it doesn't have to look big or fancy to become the most popular, comfortable, or memorable room in the house. But as much as those old looks have their retro charm, our expectations of these spaces have changed. **The family room has grown up.**

The opportunity to create more considered, more stylish environments always excites me, but when it comes to the family room, it should ride high on comfort and fun and low on pretense. It needs to feel truly casual, a place to kick back with the fam and enjoy being together.

You can design this secondary living area around entertainment: binge-watching TV; game gatherings, or create a quieter lounge for conversation and connection, maybe even a little light reading.

A great family room should stand up to more wear and tear than living rooms, so it needs durable, aesthetically pleasing materials that are easy to keep clean, such as stone, hardwoods, area rugs, and indoor-outdoor, stain-free fabrics. Design strategies and storage solutions should make tidying up supereasy, including doors on shelving to hide rogue wires and instruction manuals; affordable but attractive baskets and bins to hold magazines, toys, and remote controls; and trays and covered boxes to keep tabletops tidy. In my household, we eat in the family room every week, including casual, comfort-food dinners and plenty of finger foods and snacks during our favorite shows. **This space always needs a large coffee table for serving and eating.** If space permits, adding a small dining table with chairs also makes good sense.

TV SOLUTIONS

Perfect Placement for the Screen

For seated TV viewers, place the center of the screen at eye level, about 42 inches from the floor. Sometimes, it needs to go higher—wall-mounted above a fireplace *perhaps*—but for the sake of your neck and others', try to avoid a situation that leads to craning. Make sure your viewing distance is 1 to 1½ times the screen size.

Next, can you easily reach an outlet, or will you need a mess of extension cords? Threading cabling through sheetrock takes effort but looks great. Otherwise, think about running cables out of sight through cupboards or, if no other option, make it a feature, using colored or braided cables.

Consider natural light and how it changes throughout the day. Will direct light or reflections bother you when watching your favorite show? Will you need shutters, blinds, or blackouts? Will that statement light fixture and table lamps glare off the screen? Lighting should be adjustable, having a low, moody quality and a bright option, too, for games, eating, and cleaning up.

If you want to hide your screen away when not in use, consider placing it in a large vintage bureau or cupboard with a sliding panel, anything you like as long as you allow for proper ventilation at the back.

Consider natural light and how it changes throughout the day. Will reflections bother you when watching your favorite show?

SOFT BUT STRONG

Tough, Hard-Wearing Fabrics That Work Perfectly in Family Rooms

Below: I used this folky stripe Poem Apple fabric for a chair I designed for Spectra Home . . .

Right: . . . and I clad the ottoman I designed in this pale blue Navigator Mineral fabric.

STORAGE SOLUTIONS

Slam Dunk in the Basket

Clutter kills fun, particularly in the family room, where people sprawl with snacks, drinks, toys, and games. **In this space, you can't have too many baskets.** Use large ones to store blankets, pillows, and toys. You can put houseplants—large and small, still in their garden-center plastic pots—into baskets. Covered boxes hold items that you want at hand but don't necessarily want to see when not in use, such as small electronics, remote controls, and extra batteries.

Surprise Guests

Stowed under a sofa table, **storage ottomans can do double duty as extra seating**. Use the space inside them to stash items that you don't want to see in open baskets, such as extra bedding (in case your family room moonlights as a guest room), plastic toys (usually in bright colors that clash with pretty much every interior), and extra cords and cables.

Shelf Life

If budget and space allow, add bookshelves, some with open shelves and some with doors, to store board games, paperwork, and, oh yeah, books. Make it interesting and keep the open shelves open with small pieces of artwork or sculpture, fresh flowers, and personal items from your past or travels.

Home Stories

MAKING IT YOURS

We didn't want this family space to look like just another cookie-cutter lounge. The homeowners liked the idea of fun and whimsy, as did the kids of course, which contrasted nicely with the gorgeous formality of the rest of the house. The paintwork for the entire space went to a rich olive with added cabinetry in deep purple, both superwarm and cozy tones. Individual zones cater to TV and gaming, plus a wet bar. Custom pennants display the whole family's initials, alongside animal heads, two seating areas, a secret play-nook, and some of the best trim work of my career. This space proves that **the family room can take a brave, eye-catching look**. As long as you design with comfort and authenticity in mind and don't feel as though you need to follow the latest trend, be as brave and bold as you like.

Use trim to frame artworks . . . or animal heads!

Paint color: Sherwin Williams Ripe Olive

If your living space is more refined, your family room can easily be as bold and unique as you like.

OFF THE KITCHEN

The family wanted to spend time in this secondary lounge space, off the kitchen, so it needed to feel fun and comfortable with a focus on the fireplace. (They eventually put a TV in place of the art.) Designed for lying down and lounging, the big, dueling sofas, three- or four-seaters, perfectly deliver that opportunity. They're so deep that, if you removed the back pillows, two people easily could lie side by side and snuggle—and who doesn't want that?

LET YOUR FURNITURE DO THE WORK

This space breaks so many of my rules, and I love it. It's an all-white rarity, and no overhead light fixture draws the eye. But everything else in the room has so much richness. **Even in a tight, white space, you can achieve real personality with the right furniture.** The recess into the walls, left and right of the window, and the custom, poured cast-stone fireplace area feel supermodern. Don't you just love the showy tufted-leather club design chairs?

Even in a tight, white space you can achieve real personality.

Delightfully impractical, daybeds are perfect for secondary living spaces.

DUELING DAYBEDS

This enormous mansion had fallen into major disrepair. It had some wonderful period detailing, but I couldn't save it all. In the family room, the blue-and-white Delft tiling around the fireplace was too far gone. Giving the existing wooden fireplace this gorgeous, rich tone set the mood for the room, which we painted in fresh hues. The black iron windows cost a fortune to repair, but I'm so glad I did it because they look stunning. The two daybeds invite coziness, which is key to the family room aesthetic.

THE DREAM SOFA

This delightful space already had tons of natural light with all these great windows, but it had too much sharp geometry, all long lines, angles, and squares. The curved club chairs and curved couch softened an otherwise harsh room. Something about the shape of that couch, you just know that you're going to slump on it later—and I love that.

CHECKLIST

- ☐ Consider your family room's primary uses—TV, games, home bar, reading—and design accordingly.
- ☐ Measure carefully for perfect TV placement.
- ☐ Think soft but strong furniture and always include a large coffee table.
- ☐ Create a sofa setup that encourages togetherness.
- ☐ Honor your family's personality or story with photos, trophies, and other items that evoke special memories.
- ☐ Overthink storage and organization.
- ☐ Hide those cables wherever possible.

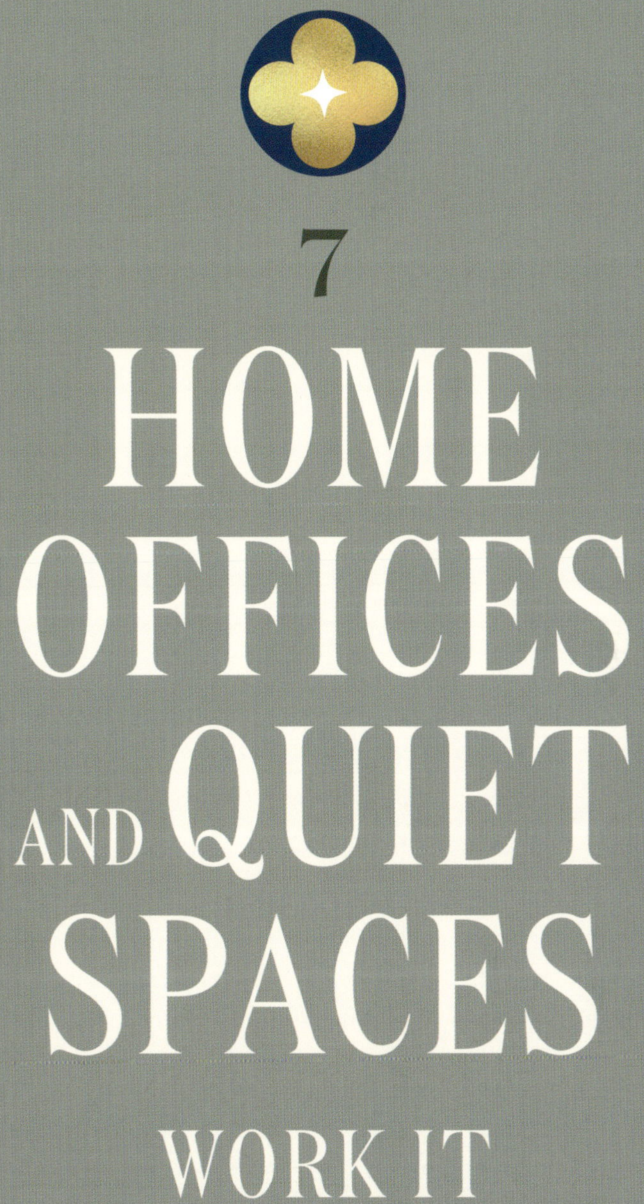

7

HOME OFFICES AND QUIET SPACES

WORK IT

The way we work has changed. In 2020, so many of us found ourselves suddenly homebound, working from makeshift setups: the kitchen counter, the vanity in the guest room, on the bed with a pillow for a desk, even just a laptop propped up in the yard. In terms of home design, this change, sudden as it was, had upsides. Many of us have returned to our original workplaces, dividing our time between home and office more than ever. Bespoke WFH (work-from-home) areas—personalized, comfortable, and beautiful—are becoming incredibly popular. Many homes now have a dedicated room, area, or nook for use as a home office. But it shouldn't look lifted from a downtown high-rise. I can't tell you how many times I've yanked enormous, impersonal, 1990s-style veneer-wood module desk-and-shelving units from home offices, replacing them with unique, stand-alone desks, functional yet attractive chairs, and bookshelves. We spend so much of our lives working that we owe it to ourselves to aim for something perfect. **Ditch the dull grays and beiges of corporate cubicles in favor of calming or rich colors, smart lighting, comfort, and living things.** These spaces need functionality, sure, but they also need to reflect your personality and working habits and to maintain the easy, relaxed style of the rest of your home.

My handy-dandy checklist, "How to Style Any Room" (page 73), applies to these spaces, too, because your working space should beckon you even when you really don't feel like burning the midnight oil to finish that report due tomorrow. The right design can make going to the "office" a joy even if your commute lasts only a few feet!

DESK

Working It

Before you think about the look and feel of your desk area, focus on function. Desks usually sit 28 to 30 inches high, but those 2 inches can mean the difference between performance perfection and a lot of back and shoulder pain. **Use a desk height calculator online to determine the right desk height for your height.** You also need to be able to sit comfortably without banging your knees, and the piece should have as few sharp edges as possible.

To protect your neck and avoid eyestrain, make sure that, when you're sitting comfortably, the top of your screen sits a touch above eye level, about an arm's length away. To achieve the right placement, use a monitor, laptop stand, or a stack of your favorite coffee table books—including this one! No room for a separate monitor? For laptop users, invest in a separate keyboard and mouse or trackpad. Your back and neck will thank you.

It's hard for me to stay in one position for too long, and science keeps telling us that we need to keep moving our bodies. So I'm a big fan of the sit-stand desk, which conforms instantly to your mood. Feeling restless? Push back your chair and raise the desk. Need a breather? Lower it and take a load off. It's a boredom-breaker and wonderful for your body.

In larger homes, where you can devote an entire room to your work zone, you can have an expansive, clutter-free desk. If you have the luxury of facing the window or a wall, choose your preference, but remember that, like sofa placement in your living space, **the desk doesn't need to kiss a wall**. You might want the option of moving around it easily. Editing your desktop objects to a handful of essentials will help keep your mind clear and focused (more on that later). In a larger space, a secondary surface works great for laying out plans, organizing presentations and paperwork, and so on. If you regularly need a printer, keep it close but consider concealing it inside a cabinet, especially if your office room hosts other functions or tasks. Why? **When was the last time you saw a pretty printer?**

For medium spaces that take up a portion of a room or hallway, install a writing desk (a little larger than a console table, with drawers), an attractive secretary, or tall bureau with built-in storage and a fold-down desk surface. For small spaces and nooks, consider a corner desk, or a two-tier fold-down desk that you can hide in a closet or behind the sofa. If you happen to have a walk-in closet, you might even repurpose that.

For tiny spaces, where your work area doubles as a kitchen surface, dining table, and puzzle corner, use a lacquered tray (to hold your keyboard and mouse, notebook and pens) or a leather desk mat to define your area clearly and to signal that it's worktime.

Pro Tip

At the end of the working day, close the door, shut the desk, or pack away your things. Those actions pack a psychological punch and help you focus on some well-earned after-work fun or relaxation.

Add a deep floating shelf to a nook and you've made an instant office.

CHAIR

A rolling office chair makes moving around the space easier. You can find so many stylish options today that you have no excuse to settle for a boring black chair on black plastic wheels. Office chairs come in bright pink leather, stately mahogany, sleek chrome and canvas, and even a wide, armless upholstered chair for sitting cross-legged.

Always test-drive an office chair in a store or pore over the reviews, especially resale listings, to see whether you've met your match. For larger spaces, secondary seating allows for a much-needed change of scene. A bistro table, window seat or banquette, or even a chaise can bring further delight and encourages you to move around as you work.

Measure up so the arms of your office chair fit easily under your desk.

NOOKS

The Smallest Spaces

Let's talk nooks. **If you don't have much space, your budget can go farther.** Splurge on a single roll of luxury wallpaper or perhaps some high-end hardware. In a tiny area, those flourishes make a lot of impact for not a lot of money. For me, the design fun happens in nooks, from superslouchy reading corners with endless pillows and throws to functional home office spaces. Here, a marble counter and sink, a steel backsplash powder-coated in a custom copper finish, and an integrated minifridge make this coffee station feel strategically luxe. Art deco wallpaper adds a little Gatsby style. It's the breakroom that you never knew you wanted.

Pro Tip

Nooks can flip the script, too. For a home office that consists of an entire room, carve out a corner for a museum moment: a piece of artwork, a design lamp, or a thrifted or antique table. If you go with a table, stage it with something living—in this case, an olive tree. Look at this gorgeous, beveled, three-dimensional trim work!

I wanted a hotel suite vibe with this nook and love its five-star look.

RUG

A Magic Carpet Ride

Instead of a thick or long-pile rug, **use a low-pile rug in your office space**. A wheeled chair glides more easily across hardworking, flat-woven rugs. The right rug will add warmth, color, and texture to the room. For large spaces, an area rug should underscore all the furniture but stop a foot or so from the edges of the room. For medium or small spaces, use a rug to zone your working area, focusing it on the desk, with a couple of feet to spare so your chair doesn't keep getting stuck on the edge.

Pro Tip

Office chair mats look so, well, office-like. A well-chosen rug makes your home office look more like a home.

LIGHTING

Light It Up Like a Boss

No surprises here, layer your lighting from multiple sources. Balance windows that flood the room with natural light with sconces and desk lamps.

Here, smart LED bulbs really come into their own. If you spend your days in (endless) video conferences, these products make a huge difference. From a phone app, you can set them to different brightness and temperature levels, from cool daylight to warm candlelight. For the average-size home office, invest in two or three and place them separately to create a rich, inviting environment with lots of depth.

Cameras can prove so unforgiving. If you want to look your best for video meetings, light yourself head-on, with a warm-toned light source close to the camera. From a window or a table lamp, side lighting can look as harsh as overhead lighting. Ring lighting, especially a dimmable 12- to 16-inch model, can help you look amazing, but remember to take a break to rest your eyes.

My StyleCraft table lights are designed to look like a piece of art for your desk.

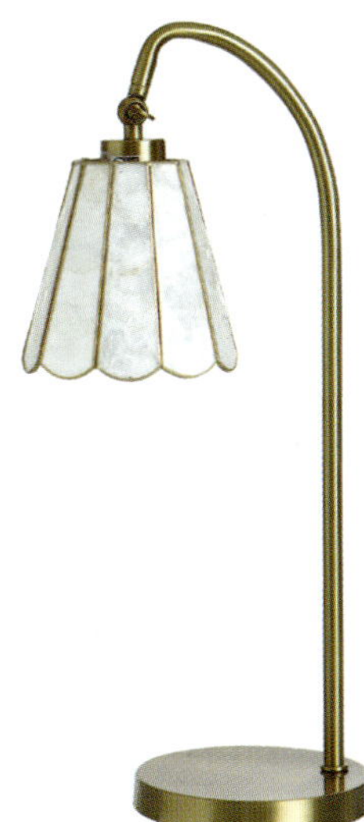

BACKDROP

What Are You Looking At?

Are the pillows straight? Did you leave your takeout wrapper on the coffee table? Wait, are those gym socks drying on the heater? Designing a background for video meetings almost never happened even a decade ago. Now we all think about it, and we can't help wonder about those fake backdrops. (*What are they hiding?*) Considering your video background, tidying it a little, and lighting it well will give a good impression. Beyond that, follow my checklist, "How to Style Any Room" (page 73). For this purpose, though, less can often work better than more, so try combining lines in the formula; for example, something old *and* wooden, or something soft *and* weird.

Your own view matters just as much. My focus and concentration depend on a plain, quiet vista not facing a window or a large, busy space. For you, the opposite might help with inspiration.

A room with two views: inspiring greenery outside and retro patterned wallpaper inside. It works!

POWER

Turn It Up

If you can add extra outlets to your workspace, do it! Plug in everything that might need some juice: your computer, lamps, chargers, space heater, small television or radio, and other electronics. Here, more than most spaces, cord control matters. **Extra outlets generally mean fewer extension cables and wires on display**, so be generous with them.

STORAGE SOLUTIONS

Filing It All Away

Depending on your personal style, and much like your kitchen and pantry cabinets, you can install storage that's open, closed, or both. Bookshelves make sense and look great as a backdrop, but so does built-in or modular shelving for pretty file boxes or baskets to pack away your paperwork. Vintage store fittings, practical and gorgeously aged, work well here, too.

PERSONAL TOUCHES

Add small elements that speak to your likes and interests, to you as a person. Make good use of artwork and such details as color, pattern, and personal objects, including awards, trophies, diplomas, and family photos. Remembering what you've achieved already, for whom you're doing it, or just a happy, fun moment that inspires you can help motivate your work.

TEMPERATURE

A Home Office Essential

Sitting still for long periods of time can lower your body temperature, no matter where you live. If your winters run supercold, like in Kansas, make a space heater or electric throw nonnegotiable for your space. No one wants to work when it feels too hot, either. A small desk fan can keep you cool and circulate air so it doesn't feel stuffy. Think about and calibrate the temperature in your home office to make it feel as comfortable as possible.

Pro Tip

Creative shelving adds visual interest (remember, your home office doesn't have to look bland and corporate), especially as a video call backdrop.

Home Stories

THE RED ROOM

A doctor originally built this house and installed a conservatory to grow medicinal plants. Built-in steam outlets kept the space temperate. Antique tiling ran across the floor and about 2 feet up the wall. Those tiles—yellow, red, blue, and green—served as the creative jumping-off point for the color scheme. The space became a home office with a bold red botanical print wallpaper for the ceiling. It felt risky, but it's one of my most daring and delightful spaces. I completely love it.

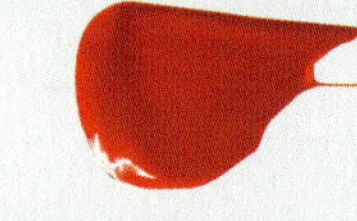

Paint color: Sherwin Williams Tanager

FRESH AND BRIGHT

Sometimes, the simplest ideas are most effective. This home office sits right off the front door, bathed in a ton of natural light from a set of giant sliding doors. The desk floats in the center of the space so two people can use it at the same time, and the calm, minimal lines of the cantilever chair match the metalwork. Note the simple area rug with its origami bird design.

Pro Tip

For open and airy office concepts, make sure your desk has plenty of built-in storage to keep the space clutter-free.

THE INFAMOUS GREEN PAINT

A single paint color, even used sparingly, can transform a space. This bold, unique, milky green reminded me of something luxe that Martha Stewart might use. Perhaps not this *exact* shade, but it created an uplifting, slightly whimsical atmosphere in this otherwise formal office. (I'm sure Martha would approve.) The color carried through to the baseboards, window frame, and French doors into a kitchen. A tonal gray print wallpaper added quiet texture, and a beige armchair in the corner offers secondary seating for a moment away from the desk (or a quiet nap when no one's looking).

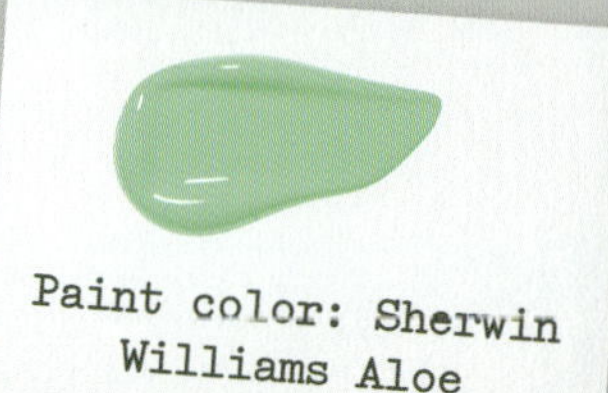

Paint color: Sherwin Williams Aloe

UNDER THE STAIRS

I almost always open living spaces, but sometimes I close them a little. This jaw-droppingly open-plan house had a dead zone under the grand staircase. It hosted only a Christmas tree, sitting empty the rest of the year. Adding the wall created an intentional nook under the stairs where the kids could read and do their homework. It instantly became an everyday part of the house, and it looks adorable.

Get creative in those rarely used spaces.

CLUBHOUSE

In this historic home, the office space needed a functioning fireplace (electric, but you can't tell), white glass tiles, and clubhouse-like trim that my dad helped me install before we painted it a rich, deep blue. Art-light sconces covered the walls, just waiting for the owner to install awards and art pieces. The dark woodwork of the two club chairs balanced the natural light coming from two sides of the room. In this renovation, a decrepit mantle above the fireplace cut into valuable space in the tiny home office. Removing the mantle, flattening the fireplace, and keeping the look mattered. It's not a real fireplace obviously, but it still feels interesting. From all three windows, bright light pours into the small space. With white tile and white ceiling, it nicely holds the rich, dark weight of Benjamin Moore Hale Navy paint. For even more personality, A. J. Cosgrove, a lamp-making artist friend, and I drilled holes in thrifted books and ran wiring through them to make a gorgeous hanging book light (books + something weird).

CHECKLIST

- ☐ Your dream desk should look great, sit at the perfect height, have lots of room underneath, and (if possible) transform to a standing desk.
- ☐ Invest in a luxe rolling chair with good back support. Consider secondary seating for a change of pace.
- ☐ For scooting that chair, use low-pile rugs, which counterbalance calmer, more focused environments.
- ☐ Layer your lighting and plan for being on-camera.
- ☐ Take the time to design the backdrop for your video meetings.
- ☐ Showcase items that reflect your personality, achievements, and inspirations.
- ☐ Keep temperature in mind because comfort helps you focus.
- ☐ Power up with extra outlets and hide those cables.
- ☐ Add sleek and simple storage so you can tidy away your working day.

8

BEDROOMS

GET SOME REST

We all need a good night's rest for our bodies to repair themselves and for emotional well-being. Bedrooms function as places to escape from the pressures of the day. (If you've heard a teenager slam a door, you know what I mean!) Bedrooms also should serve as sanctuaries. Everyone needs private time and private space: to stare at the ceiling, dream and unwind, pose in the mirror, read a book, gossip with friends, scroll online, and watch endless videos. For new parents, other caregivers, and the overworked, these spaces can offer a real lifeline. Design remains integral to all those purposes. It's not just about picking the right mattress, blackout blinds, and lighting system but also layout, color scheme, incidental furniture, soft touches, and thoughtful little details that make the space perfect for decompressing, journaling, pillow fights, or whatever suits your fancy.

My own bedroom has a great mattress, good lighting, and wallpaper in a soft cream and beige buffalo check that conveys the right amount of visual interest without making me go cross-eyed. Reading, which I do more in my bedroom than any other room, has informed the design. The room features bookshelves, a vintage English-style reading table with turned pedestal, and a cabinet in the hallway where read books live, close by, before I donate them. The room showcases my display of snow globes collected over the years, and my favorite framed artworks lean casually against the wall. My husband, Bill, always asks when I'm going to hang them. I'm not, they look great as they are! It's the calmest, coziest room in the house.

My design clients on *Bargain Mansions* and beyond love special elements in these airy, inviting environments, from a gorgeous coffee bar that gave the room the feel of a hotel suite to a hidden refrigerator drawer full of sodas and seltzers. If you have the space and the budget, don't hold back on making this room as personal as you like. **Nail the functionality, get the design right, and you'll be ready for bed in no time.**

LIGHTING

Creating a Calming Atmosphere

Work with natural light, lamps, and can lights to create a perfectly harmonious, layered lighting system. Soft, warm lighting creates a soothing atmosphere, and can lights have their use, too, especially when you need extra brightness for dressing, changing bedding, or cleaning. Different light sources allow you to control the amount of light based on what you're doing. **Have a light source next to the bed and overhead lighting as well.** Overhead lighting can include can lights or a dramatic hanging fixture: chandelier, pendant, or otherwise. A floor lamp next to a chair gives you a great little moment for a beverage and a book.

If, like me, you like reading in your bedroom, lighting needs special consideration. Nightstand lamps are fine, but **consider installing a pair of sconces or pendant lights, hung low with the bulb out of your eyeline when sitting in bed**, as strong alternatives. This approach works great in smaller spaces or if you need more surface area on your nightstands.

Adjustable lighting—lamps, sconces, spotlights—also make a clever addition. Color temperature matters, too. Bulbs should give warm tones, and smart bulbs more than do the job. If you go for sconces or pendants, you'll need switches or a dimmer within arm's reach. Otherwise, you have to get up when all cozy to turn off the light? No thanks.

COLORS AND WALLPAPERS

The Starting Point for Any Room Design

A good color story moves through a whole home, with moments of contrast of course, but bedrooms deserve special consideration. My design checklist, "How to Style Any Room" (page 73), applies to all bedrooms and guest rooms, but **pick a color scheme that soothes you**. For me, that's warm beiges and cream tones. The most popular hue, a pale, calming blue, looks fresh and inviting when paired with off-white, but you probably already know which colors make you feel calm. From that starting point, add wallpaper, trim, an upholstered headboard, drapes, and more with lots of visual interest—but with an overall vibe of personal comfort.

This metallic kaleidoscope wallpaper I designed is pure laid-back luxe.

SOFT STUFF

Sleep-Well Essentials

When sitting in bed, I lean against at least two firm pillows, and soft pillows gently support my head and make for nice hugging at night. We spend so much of our lives sleeping that we owe it to ourselves to make the experience good. **The average pillow lasts only a couple of years before it needs replacing.** Cycling your pillows can ward off dust mites and allergies.

Invest some time and do your research. For example, **the softest linen sometimes can prove the least hard-wearing.** But don't get too sidetracked with thread counts. If your bedding is 100 percent natural, containing little to no manufactured fibers, you'll sleep like a dream, whichever the season.

For each bedroom, choose and stick to the same bedding base layer. Find a good-quality base sheet and some pillowcases that you love and invest in a few versions. If you feel like a change or the season requires it, swap the pillows for shams, add a Belgian linen eiderdown, a Pendleton blanket, or even a classic American folk-art quilt from Etsy. You instantly get a different look without having to buy a whole new bed set.

DRAPES

Layering Light and Texture

Controlling daylight through your drapes, blinds, shutters, and window treatments plays a huge part in creating the perfect sleep-ready atmosphere. You can tweak the quality of light with sheer fabrics, block it completely with blackout blinds, and retain warmth via drapes with thermal lining.

Blinds offer the most control but rarely block all light. You need a solid fabric version for that, and even then, light will seep around the edges. Cellular or honeycomb shades are opaque and trap air inside their double layer, giving the setup insulation powers. The versatility of curtains plays well with blinds, and drapes generally run heavier and longer than curtains. Lots of light or none, you don't need to follow any hard-and-fast rules. You do you.

FLOORING

Luxury Underfoot

Most people go barefoot in bedrooms, dressing rooms, and walk-ins, and even those of us who adore a hardwood floor appreciate something soft and luxurious underfoot. In this low-impact, low-traffic area, consider trying more decorative, luxe floor treatments, such as parquet. For strategic softness, place rugs on either side of the bed (nothing like sinking your feet into a soft rug first thing in the morning!), en route to the bathroom, in the walk-in, and in front of a full-length mirror.

Who doesn't love classic herringbone parquet?

CLOSETS AND DRESSING AREAS

Hang in There

Designing a space just for yourself feels so special. Your guests don't see these hidden areas of your home, which can make them freeing and fascinating. My closet isn't for everyone, it's for me—and I love it.

Movies and TV shows—looking at you, *Working Girl*, *Clueless*, and *Sex and the City*—have supercharged the fantasy dressing-room ideal with gorgeous loungelike interiors, Gatsby-style decor, and boutique-level cabinetry. The dressing areas that I've created in my own design practice rank as some of my most-loved spaces. The spacious, top-tier versions have an island, handcrafted cabinetry, layered lighting with pendants and chandeliers, full-length mirrors, upholstered seating, a vintage or bespoke vanity, display cases, and even a coffee or cocktail corner.

In your closet, you might not have room for a Champagne bar or limited-edition sneaker collection, but you can incorporate elements of this laid-back luxe approach into any size space you like. In large homes, a series of walk-in closets of varying sizes allows for endless combinations. Even if you don't live in a mansion, you still can add cabinetry; drawers; a stand-alone dresser or chest of drawers; hanging organizers; or baskets, boxes, and storage bargains from a box or warehouse store.

The internal cabinetry of a closet should appear neutral: natural wood, off-white, and so on. Colorful designs, as wonderful as they might sound, will make your clothing look, well, *weird*. Vibrant paint reflects onto your clothes, making it impossible to know for sure what matches. **Use your fifth wall, the ceiling, to add a little spice.** Wallpapering the ceiling gives a fun look, and a richly toned, patterned carpet or thick, squishy rug feels elegant. In dressing rooms and large walk-ins, it's worth investing in comfortable flooring because you're more likely to go barefoot there.

This mirror, placed in front of a gorgeously arched window with privacy glass, is lit by natural light during the day and sconces at night.

In medium and small spaces, consider creating a reach-in closet, painted and trimmed to blend with its surroundings. Clothes hangers run 17 to 19 inches wide, so your closet needs to measure slightly deeper, about 24 inches or even deeper for bulky coats and winter wear. In tiny spaces, where 24 inches aren't going to work, install a series of pegs, 24 inches apart. From them, hang your coats and clothes flush against the wall.

Lighting

Hardwire a lighting system in your closets and consider smart lighting to control the temperature and brightness from your phone. Lit closet rods helpfully illuminate clothes from the top down. Make it a little brighter than you might think. You need to tell similar pieces of clothing apart, after all.

Editing and Organizing

Seasonal editing, such as stowing winter clothes until the leaves fall, sounds old-fashioned, but it's a smart strategy. Boxing or bagging and storing means that your day-to-day pieces can hang freely, making them easier to see and making it easier to put outfits together.

Practice purging and embrace resale or the donation pile. Rather than doing one big spring clean, keep on top of your closets a few times a year. Go section by section—shirts, T-shirts, other tops, and so on—rather than rummaging through everything all at once and hoping for the best before you run out of steam.

Storage

Closets and dressing areas represent a storage solution in themselves, but smaller spaces might not have a lot of closet space, let alone a walk-in. But you can add storage anywhere. Beds, benches, window seats, chairs, and ottomans all have storage versions. After you've edited your wardrobe, use these objects to store seasonal apparel.

SEATING

For Rest and Relaxation

A lot of people overlook bedroom seating. Sure, you can sit on your bed to put on your socks and shoes, but **a bench or chair makes every layout more multifunctional and inviting**. If you have space, a firm upholstered bench or small settee at the foot of the bed works wonders and can create a small sitting area when paired with side tables or a coffee table.

Window seats and banquette seating always delight and double as storage. Impractical yet gorgeous, a chaise longue (page 63) looks great in a bedroom suite, even if you fling all your clothes on it, making it the world's most gorgeous valet or laundry pedestal. Most spaces can take at least one comfortable reading chair. Very small spaces look great with a vintage hardwood chair or stool that doubles as a side table.

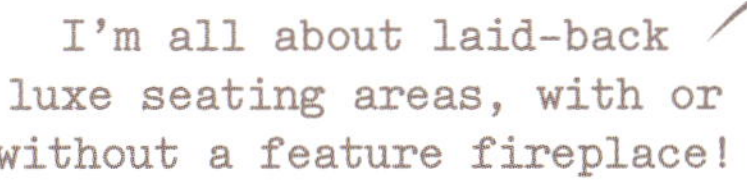

I'm all about laid-back luxe seating areas, with or without a feature fireplace!

BEDTIME MOMENTS

Designing for Life

I can't tell you how many times movie night ends up with all the kids piled on our bed on a Friday night. Whether you're seeking some solo time, together time, or family time, here's how to make your bedroom feel pleasant and cozy. **Next to the bed and next to any seat in the room, always have a space to set a glass.** A nightstand works well bedside, and you can repurpose a small cocktail table next to a chair.

Paint color: Benjamin Moore Hale Navy

A table lamp, vintage book, and blooms? Delightful.

The perfect place for your water (or martini) glass.

GUEST ROOM

Expect the Unexpected

Want to know the secret to making overnight guests feel welcome? Give them what they need: a comfortable bed, somewhere to put their belongings, a basket of clean towels, a carafe of water, and something special. **Provide a version of everything in your own room and add a little luxury:** a tray with upscale essentials, such as bathroom minis, a sleeping mask, a scented candle (Grapefruit & Mint) with a book of matches, easy-to-access charging cables, and a bedside drawer filled with useful items, including aspirin, a new toothbrush, disposable razors, and such.

In a hot or cold climate, instructions on how to tweak the temperature help. Supply extra blankets, no matter the weather or season. Finally, throw in some reading material, such as your favorite novels or magazines, and dress it all with some freshly cut flowers.

For small spaces, one beds and studios, a fold-out foam mattress wins the race to a good night's sleep for a guest. (No one, and I mean *no one*, wants to inflate a mattress at midnight.) Combine it with a mattress protector and some upscale bedding, all of which you can store under your own bed or in a closet.

KIDS' BEDROOMS

Start with What They Love

Depending on their age, children and young people need different design in their rooms. Right now, my sons need a place to put all their empty bowls of mac and cheese! A big hamper keeps the floor space clear until laundry day. Lots of hangers make returning clean clothes to the closet easier (no promises). **Hooks can work *miracles* in kids' rooms.** My sons find it easier to hang something on a hook than a hanger.

Address functionality first and then center their passions. Some kids' rooms clearly have taken incredible effort, but making them pretty can prove challenging because . . . how far do you go? What happens if your child loses interest in the current obsession?

One solution frames their interests—literally. Shadow boxes, picture frames deep enough to hold objects, make a great option. Frame a favorite band T, jersey, baseball glove, even a deflated basketball. Anything goes. The frame elevates its contents, so put something weird and personal on display, such as a much-loved pair of sneakers. Another display hack that gives sense and structure to a child's room consists of thinking in multiples. One jar of marbles or a little matchbox toy car looks fine, but three or five look even better. A baseball bat looks okay on a wall, but a row of them, with jars of baseballs nearby, looks impactful. It may be your home, but your child's bedroom is your child's bedroom. If they show interest, include them in the design process.

snuggle

Home Stories

MAKING IT A FEATURE

This nook felt like the weirdest little space. I wanted to incorporate it into the room, but there was no way to straighten the wall, especially with electrical cabling behind it, so it became a feature. Floating shelves add a lot to the room. As you enter, you see them first, and they offer a good example of knowing when to compromise. If you're flexible with your design, you can come up with some pretty solutions. **Make an unwanted nook or niche a feature.** In a larger room, add a comfortable chair, side table, floating shelves, bespoke storage, or sconce lighting. One or more of those strategies will do the trick in any size space.

In this naturally bright room, facing the bed away from the window gave my clients a little privacy.

DON'T HOLD BACK

In this historic house, we vaulted into the attic for a giant, dramatic, angled slope to this bedroom, washing all the walls in a beautiful, rich, earthy beige. In addition to the trim detailing, the room features unique elements, from oddly shaped windows unified with loud drapes by Kelly O'Neil that, of course, I love, to a lush headboard with huge tufting and a high, ornate, romantic back. The hardwood flooring was original to the room. Fun historical fact: 1-inch boards, rather than 3-inch, allow for better expansion and contraction during the hottest and coldest months.

Paint color: Farrow and Ball Dead Salmon

With such a dramatic view, I chose cool and muted tones for the upholstery and rug.

CELEBRATING WHAT YOU HAVE

This huge, beautiful bay window needed a bedroom design that embraced it. So much natural light flooded the room, and the grand house has such a beautiful backyard. The window had to become the focal point. The soffit had to stay because of ductwork, but adding electrical allowed for these Moroccan pendant lights. **Pendants above nightstands free up valuable surface area.** A watercolor print wallpaper on the ceiling and soffit continued above the windows, making it feel like the soffit detail went all the way around the room. Reinstalling the original dining room crystal chandelier caught the light, and two tufted chairs in the bay are perfect for morning coffee or a glass of wine at golden hour.

BOLDNESS IN SMALLER SPACES

Can you go bold in a smaller space? For sure! This wallpaper, with its bright and bold botanic print, had the power to transform this once-plain main bedroom and make it feel more intimate if other elements created calmer contrast. The print and the lattice effect of the headboard in a soft bone color harmonize perfectly and wouldn't work as well if the headboard had a crazy color, too. Luxurious fabrics add a little extra laid-back, slouchy luxury.

WORKING WITH UNIQUE SHAPES

This huge, rambling house already had so many fantastic details. They just needed to sing. This sweeping barrel ceiling was original to the main bedroom and unusual for its size, especially in Kansas City, where I've never seen another one. The barrel measured 8 feet at the bottom but 10 at its highest point, which made for some interesting design work-arounds. In the end, painting the walls in charcoal and edging them in white underlined it as a feature. The headboard stayed low, the graphic rug echoed the wall color, and a modern light fixture respectfully nodded to leaded-and-steel windows original to the house.

Pro Tip

An upholstered blanket box or bench at the foot of the bed is a must: It's functional seating by day and a place to store extra blankets and pillows for family movie nights.

THE PERFECT BEDROOM

This rich-toned, high-gloss bedroom in a century-old stone home proved challenging. The tight space had a small walk-in closet, an aging bathroom next door, and hardly any room to walk around the bed. Taking out the closet added 4 feet to the length of the room, and getting rid of the bath created a walk-through closet and laundry room with natural light. Adding space and functionality, a tough decision, meant making the main bedroom completely gorgeous. Historic detailing included trim work, incorporating a fixed headboard, a warm metal light fixture, and sconces over a couple of tight little nightstands. Adding layers of stone to the fireplace with a tapered black marble finish created a dramatic focal point. The deep blue gloss and dark brown hardwood floor fit the era, and I love the fireplace safety guard with its offbeat, natural design. **Sometimes, that one crazy item can make a space.**

Paint color: Farrow and Ball De Nimes

Pro Tip

Dark paint colors come alive with a gloss finish; the subtle reflections add to your layered lighting design.

BLACK AS AN ANCHOR

Paint color: Sherwin Williams Tricorn Black

This room cried out for drama. It had lots of natural light with a sliding glass door, another big window, and the sweeping rise to the ceiling. The family loved black, and I loved their bold choice. I add natural wood to most of the spaces that I create, so with a limited budget, I added a strip of wood trim as a fun architectural detail to pick up on the house's midcentury vibe. **Painting a space black always feels like a bold move, but something magical happens** when dressing the room: all other colors pop. Art, fabric, sheets, pillows, tchotchkes, even clothes will stand out.

THE WORLD'S BIGGEST WINDOW

Regular residential windows don't come in this size, but the view looked so stunning and the room so big that it was crying out for something breathtaking. This special-order, custom window brought in a beautiful view of this ginormous estate where deer walk in the mornings. The yellowing, 1980s wood ceiling looked great toned down and washed with an opaque white stain. We kept it simple on the walls with a super subtle, tone on tone, beige-and-white paper, which creates a horizontal line that mimics the line of the ceiling and goes all the way around the room, even into the secondary lounge space with a fireplace now clad with natural stone—a gorgeous place to sit and relax.

The room was so big it was crying out for something breathtaking.

THE THREE-TIER CLOSET

This house was a real knockout, both visually and because demolition gave me a black eye! Removing a tough piece of trim suddenly jammed it in my eye. **Always, *always* wear safety goggles, folks.** Removing a wall created this humongous walk-in closet with three levels of storage. Such a grand space had to have a great ceiling treatment: a beautiful gold-and-white paper. Again, neutral-toned cabinetry works perfectly for closets because louder colors can change how your clothing looks.

TINY AND TOO CUTE

In this home, the owner had set up temporary racks here because the main bedroom had no storage. Reconfiguring the entire upper floor took a little space from the main bedroom to expand a bathroom and reworked this onetime guest bedroom into a small, superluxe dressing room. This intentional space gave her the functionality and fun she was seeking. For me, it's all about the glamorous light fitting and the cute kaleidoscope-inspired wallpaper on the ceiling. The room has good natural light, so a subtle UV tint to the window (just out of shot) provided privacy and protection for her clothing.

Pro Tip

Consider reworking your bedroom layout to incorporate a dressing area. Any floor space you might lose in the main room, you'll make up for with this truly practical storage area that has limitless cute potential.

LIGHTING WHAT YOU LOVE

This client wanted her own luxe closet space separate from her husband's. Fun and glam, she loved bags and shoes and wanted to enjoy her accessories even when not wearing them. Display cabinetry, an upholstered storage bench, and an LED lighting system elevated her favorite possessions. **Add lighting strips to any kind of meaningful collection or storage:** silk ties, jewelry, limited-edition sneakers, whatever's precious to you. This star-shaped beaded pendant light felt like just the right amount of glam without going over the top.

CHECKLIST

- ☐ Layer your lighting to set yourself up for successful sleep. Control temperature and color.
- ☐ Start with naturally soothing tones and build on them.
- ☐ Low traffic means dream flooring, but have something soft underfoot.
- ☐ Add seating to bedrooms for true comfort.
- ☐ Go wild with hidden spaces such as closets and dressing areas.
- ☐ Give guests what they need: comfort, a functional space, and something special.
- ☐ Incorporate your kids' passions and get them involved.

9 BATHROOMS

IT'S SPA TIME

Marble, glass, or ceramic; handmade far away; vintage and reclaimed; in every shape and formation imaginable: More tile is good tile (though my crew and contractors might disagree when we're grouting late into the night!). You can tile other areas of the home, but in the bathroom you can go truly tile crazy. Tile has a functionality essential in the wet and wild environment of the bathroom, a space that you need to clean regularly and with ease, but the limitless, endlessly pretty choices are exciting! Grouting can work in almost any color, but when it comes to floor tiles, pick an off-white or dark tone. Charcoal gray goes with almost anything. Pure white will stain. With smaller, handmade tiles consider running them tightly against one another.

Most bathroom spaces run small, so designing one gives you a chance to indulge some serious decor fantasies using cabinetry, hardware, lighting, wallpaper, fabric, and fixtures. You can do all that on a more reasonable scale and without breaking the budget. Again, functionality takes the lead. What do you need? Will you need a separate shower (probably), or are you fine showering in the tub? Do you need a tub at all?—keeping in mind that every home should have (at least) one. Is one basin enough, or do you need more? A double vanity, with its two basins, has saved many a marriage. Do you need special fixtures for easy cleaning, such as an extra, removable showerhead? Does an electronic Japanese-style toilet with an AI bidet sound like a good idea?

With a few strategic trade-offs, you can achieve a high-end look that fits your budget. For example, pair stock cabinetry—less expensive than custom-made—with high-end pulls, knobs, and countertops for a bespoke feeling. Elevate plate-glass mirrors or plain cabinets with painted or stained wood trim to look like an expensive, handcrafted piece.

Perhaps your dream bathroom means business, no frills, and that's fine, but you still have a real design opportunity here. For lighting, look at chandeliers and sconces marketed for other rooms. Use wallpaper as you would wainscoting and tile above it for a "designer" look at a fraction of the cost of tiling the whole room. Shower temperature controls, heat lamps, towel warmers, mood lighting, waterproof speakers, and other innovations can create an indulgent aesthetic. If your budget allows, splurge on the extra-luxe touch of a heated floor. Nothing feels as good as a warm bathroom floor on a cold morning. Some houses, because of their design or age, can't be retrofitted with this feature, so if not, add a cozy soft rug to the bathroom, which adds color and texture, too!

DECOR

Calming Tones

Again, my design checklist, "How to Style Any Room (page 73), applies here. But as with your closets, avoid strong colors that will reflect onto your skin and change its tone. Blues and greens behave worst in this area when choosing paint colors, countertops, and tiles. Use them away from mirrors or forget about color all together and go bright and white, perhaps with a few Carrara marble accents for good measure.

Pro Tip

Think about how the color tones of your decor will bounce off your skin and design accordingly, especially around a mirror.

LIGHTING

Looking Good at the Flick of a Switch

Let's look at how to layer light successfully in the bathroom. Lighting is crucial around the basin area, where the household will style hair, apply makeup, shave, and so on. Here, you'll need the option of a strong, warm-toned light source for those tasks. Create secondary lighting that offers a softer, more relaxing atmosphere for long soaks in the tub with a lit candle and a glass of wine, a perfect laid-back luxury. **Almost all my bathroom designs feature decorative sconces rather than vanity lights.** Can lights work great when you need strong, consistent brightness for cleaning, but don't rely on them for atmosphere—or for looking good in the mirror.

HARDWARE

Luxe Essentials

Tub, toilet, basin, and more can dictate much of your bathroom layout, but a few key considerations still apply. Do you want a single basin or a double vanity? Would you give up freestanding tub rights for a roomy walk-in shower?

Shower sets have come a long way: sleek, brass-toned fittings, generous showerheads, high-quality faucets, large bases, and even digital controls. It's easy to install a steam system and it's easy, pretiling, to install showers with built-in body sprays. In recent decades, sinks have undergone incredible innovation: classic wall-mounted, pedestal, and console versions with chrome plumbing; hidden undermounts, meaning the basin sits low, underneath an opening in the vanity; inset sinks; and glass or ceramic bowls or stone vessels that sit on your countertop as if just placed there. In each instance, consider ease of use. Classic fittings endure for a reason, but an undermount nicely maximizes counter space, especially if using gorgeous, hand-cut marble. A shallow, traylike modern basin will prove tricky for washing your face, but it might work for handwashing in a powder room.

Shower doors come with frames, like factory windows, or frameless for a sleek look, and toilets have seemingly endless choices now: one-piece, two-piece, wall-hung with cistern in the wall, and "smart." For a simple, elegant look, **a toilet with a square base has a little more style**. Adding a silent exhaust and heated mirrors, especially in smaller, steamy bathrooms, never hurts.

Reanimate a vintage piece for your console.

Think beyond chrome, as with this powder-coated purple shower system that contrasts with the brass-toned hose.

Is there anything more delightful than a heated bathroom floor?

TILE

The Home Designer's Delight

If you can, tile the floor and the walls around the shower and/or bath. **Use tile as wainscoting around the perimeter of the room**, into window alcoves, anywhere and everywhere. It's *so* easy to clean. **In this space, bigger is better**, especially on floors and in shower or tub enclosures, because that means fewer grout lines to keep clean. You can order large stone tiles—marble, quartz, and quartzite—in slices from the same block, which creates a dramatic design story across the space. Tiny, pretty penny tiles in circular, triangular, or other geometric shapes come on sheets for easy installation. It takes just minutes and gives a retro, elegant feel, especially on bathroom floors. Swap certain tiles in a contrast color to create a bespoke border or a set of initials. It's easier than you think. **Definitely create a tiled recessed shelf, for the ultimate laid-back luxe touch in your shower.**

POWDER ROOMS

Big Ideas for Small Spaces

For creating gorgeous, jewel-box powder rooms full of color and detail, don't hold back. If your creative side can't shine in the smallest room, then where? Bold colors, especially rich navy or even black, make every other color pop, and those same dark tones or patterned wallpaper can make a tiny powder room seem larger because they obscure the true shape and size of the room. Add some art, an eye-catching pendant light, and a huge leafy plant. You won't regret it.

STORAGE SOLUTIONS

Closed for Business

Open shelving doesn't look good in bathrooms because bathroom necessities—toothpaste, soap, shampoo, shaving cream—usually don't match, nor do they always look good. Instead, go for closed storage, such as a small linen closet, vintage dressers, or closed under-counter storage. For those who forget it if they can't see it, opt for mirrored medicine cabinets, especially when recessed into the wall. You can store all your essentials and occasionals together, knowing that you'll open it once or twice a day at least. For a hand towel always at the ready, install a towel ring, hook, or bar near the sink and use covered dishes or a small, lacquered tray for other day-to-day items.

SPECIAL TOUCHES

In larger spaces, a wooden chair or small bench fits a variety of uses, including as a place to leave your towel or phone for long podcast-in-the-tub sessions. **Small spaces benefit from decorative hooks**, and towel frames—slim, mounted, or up against the wall like a vintage train rack—look great and have good functionality, too. Washable rugs and soft flooring solutions underfoot will feel wonderful.

Home Stories

TILE AS DESIGN STATEMENT

Wet rooms save space, so I always try to add them to the bathrooms I design, even large spaces such as this one. It's unusual to be able to put a tub in front of the shower, an opportunity that I couldn't resist! The layout is striking, but the tile serves as the statement here. The design creates little pyramids in the light and a line up the wall that feels continuous and intentional. The shower had two heads for a couple, who could enter from either side. Just behind the low divider sits a window, and with those gloss tiles, the whole space glows with an incredible amount of natural light. Marble flooring, a step into the shower, and contrast black hardware added luxury. Opposite this space stands an incredible, modern 10-foot vanity, which called for bold tiling design, and floor tile climbs the back wall. LEDs backlight the mirrors, and a set of pendants and faceted vessel sinks make the whole room pop.

DAD SPA

A single dad wanted his bathroom to have a calming element so he could relax and wash off the stress of the day. Drawing inspiration from hotel spas, I went all out. In the central area, vaulting the ceiling made it twice as high, and a dark but neutral tone calmed everything down. These smooth, custom concrete floating vanities ended up weighing 400 pounds each. (The exterior framing of the house had to support them!) The center cabinet comes from IKEA, and the shower on the left has a separate steam room, with an infrared sauna on the right. In the shower, a built-in bench allows for lying down to enjoy the steam, and the modern, minimal sconces add spa-like detail.

Custom concrete and a sturdy IKEA find kept the cost low and the wow-factor high.

MODERN VINTAGE THROUGH MARBLE

This delightful house—almost all concrete, making it *extremely* challenging to remodel—had a series of space constraints. It called for a dramatic renovation but with a historic edge, which meant going with Carrara marble on the shower walls, countertop, and floor. That touch instantly lifted this small bathroom space, giving it a luxurious vibe like a boutique hotel in Europe. After that, a little grandma-chic wallpaper makes it feel timeless. Is it vintage, is it new—who knows? It just feels right. My NIX Spectro 2 gadget perfectly color-matched the wallpaper to the ceiling.

GOING OFF-LABEL

I'm not ashamed to say that penny tiles enthrall me, so imagine my excitement at finding this marble version. They appear here in a long stripe, like a runner, with pale porcelain tiles on either side. A sturdy Schluter brass trim sold as tile edging for walls went into the shower, but I also went even more off-script and embedded it in the floor for extra-luxe detail. It looks incredible. This bathroom on a budget used flat-pack furniture, but you can't tell because it reads as upscale and completely serene. It turned out so well.

QUIET LUXURY

This special client has worked with me for years, so the job required something truly amazing. We ended up with a spa-like bathroom big on marble, with sweeping archways, a barreled alcove over the tub, and another over the shower. The fabulous, unique marble backsplash has soft multicolored tones, and the secondary tile has little inset triangles of brass, with floor tiles in a herringbone formation. I custom-colored the plumbing in slate gray. Mounted on the ceiling, the awesome tub filler makes a wonderful waterfall sound. The glass bubble lights play into the classic bathroom vibe, and the lavender haze of the cabinetry adds soft contrast.

Using tonally similar tiles in one space works best when arranged in different formations.

I love the vintage bathhouse vibe of this alcove.

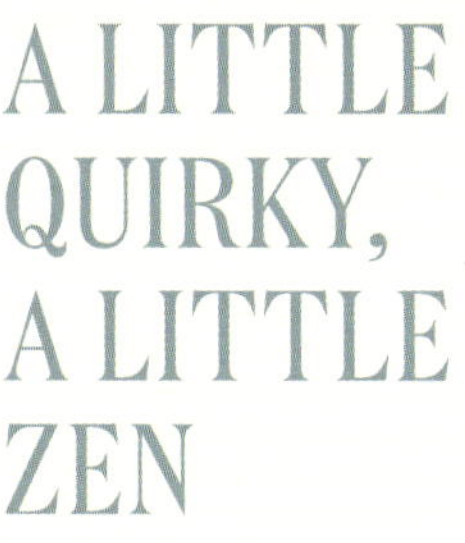

A LITTLE QUIRKY, A LITTLE ZEN

This amazing waterfall feature from the ceiling, which I wanted to do from the start, needed more of a focus, something fabulous to frame it. Cladding the walls and flooring in sheets of pebbles and selecting a rectangular tub made it all feel very Zen. A white oak box frame filled with living moss gives a surprising natural element.

MEMBERS' CLUB

This client wanted a bold, luxurious powder room, which we achieved with a huge sheet of marble with lively black-and-gray veins and rich charcoal paintwork. I chose a vintage-style pedestal sink and toilet to add to the monochromatic color story, added an extra touch of glamor with warm brass hardware and sconces, and balanced the look with a pale wood floor. The scalloped-edge mirror is my design for Varaluz. I think this powerful powder room has a VIP-members'-club vibe and the client loved its boldness.

Pro Tip

Go all-out with your powder room: It's often one of the most overlooked spaces in a home and offers incredible opportunities to surprise and delight.

SUPERLUXURIOUS

These clients wanted a wet room with lots of personality, and they also wanted the final reveal to be a surprise. No pressure! Consecutively installing lively marble cut from the same block allows the seams and veins to flow organically across the space, but functionality delivers the wow factor: two steam units powering the sauna, two showerheads, two rain heads, four body sprays, a bathtub filler and hand sprays, and a reverse air filtration ventilation system so opening the door doesn't lose steam. In the 9-foot-long infinity bath, the water constantly reheats. It's one of my most luxurious bathrooms, and the clients loved it. (Phew!)

No two blocks of marble are the same; pick one you love.

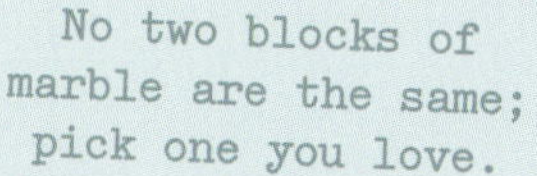

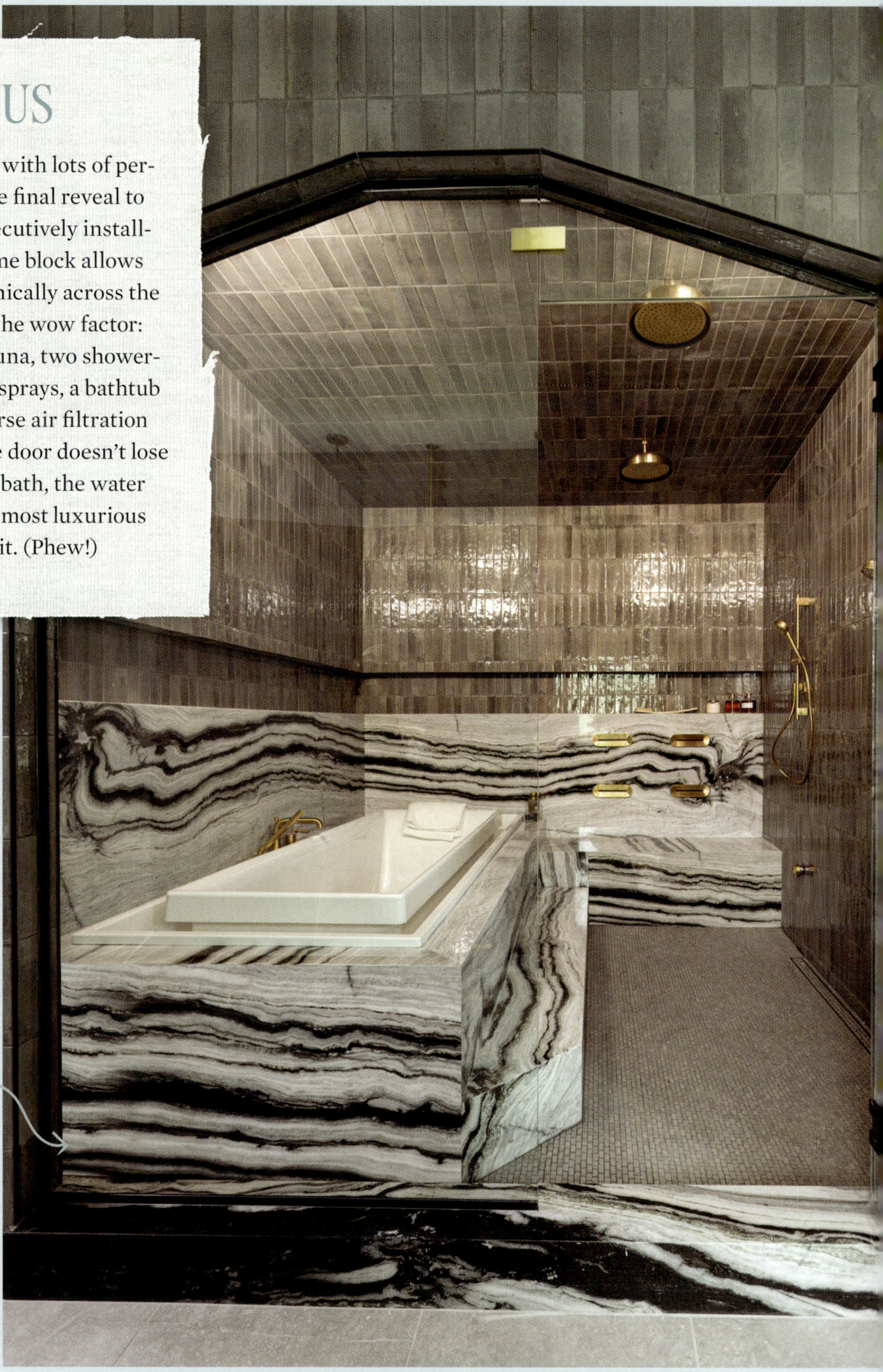

SCALLOPED VANITY

This room originally served as a doctor's small office. It had several windows and great natural light, but it faced a neighbor's white stucco wall. It became a delightful half-bath without a view but with a marble backsplash to hide part of the old windows and a scalloped edge underneath (plumbing hidden behind the lowest central point). The retro ceramic floor tile, new but designed to look vintage, forms a checkerboard pattern.

CUSTOM-MADE SOLUTION

The brief for this bathroom called for adding tons of natural light. The modern double vanity has a 3-inch-thick countertop in Tahitian cream marble in front of a wall of rain glass windows, but where to put the mirrors? Inspired by tension rods, my custom solution floated each mirror in front of the windows on slim, brass-toned poles. The walnut vanity has tons of storage, with no visible outlets because they all are hiding in the drawers. You don't have to hide *all* your outlets, but do you want endless cables in full view? Let's hope not!

THE PERFECT HALF-BATH

A mud space became this glam half-bath. The beautiful coral tone color-matched perfectly with the fabulous crane print wallpaper, the delicate custom cabinet, the hand-carved marble vessel basin on a black marble countertop, and the pair of slim sconces. But it's the floor for me. Marble checkerboard tiles appear in a playful diagonal layout, and gorgeous antique dark wood doors original to the house frame the whole thing. It's such a small but well-used space, and upscaling with marble, artisanal wallpaper, and the stone basin was totally worth it.

CHECKLIST

- ☐ Use calming, neutral tones to make you look your best.
- ☐ Overthink your vanity lighting, allow for subtle settings, and save can-lit brightness for cleaning.
- ☐ Think: function *and* fun when choosing hardware.
- ☐ You can't have too much tile, but use it wisely.
- ☐ Go bold in powder rooms and other small spaces.
- ☐ Keep storage closed to streamline your look.
- ☐ Include special touches and a little luxury (because, obviously).

SAMSUNG

10 MUDROOMS AND LAUNDRY ROOMS

OFF WITH YOUR SHOES AND SOCKS

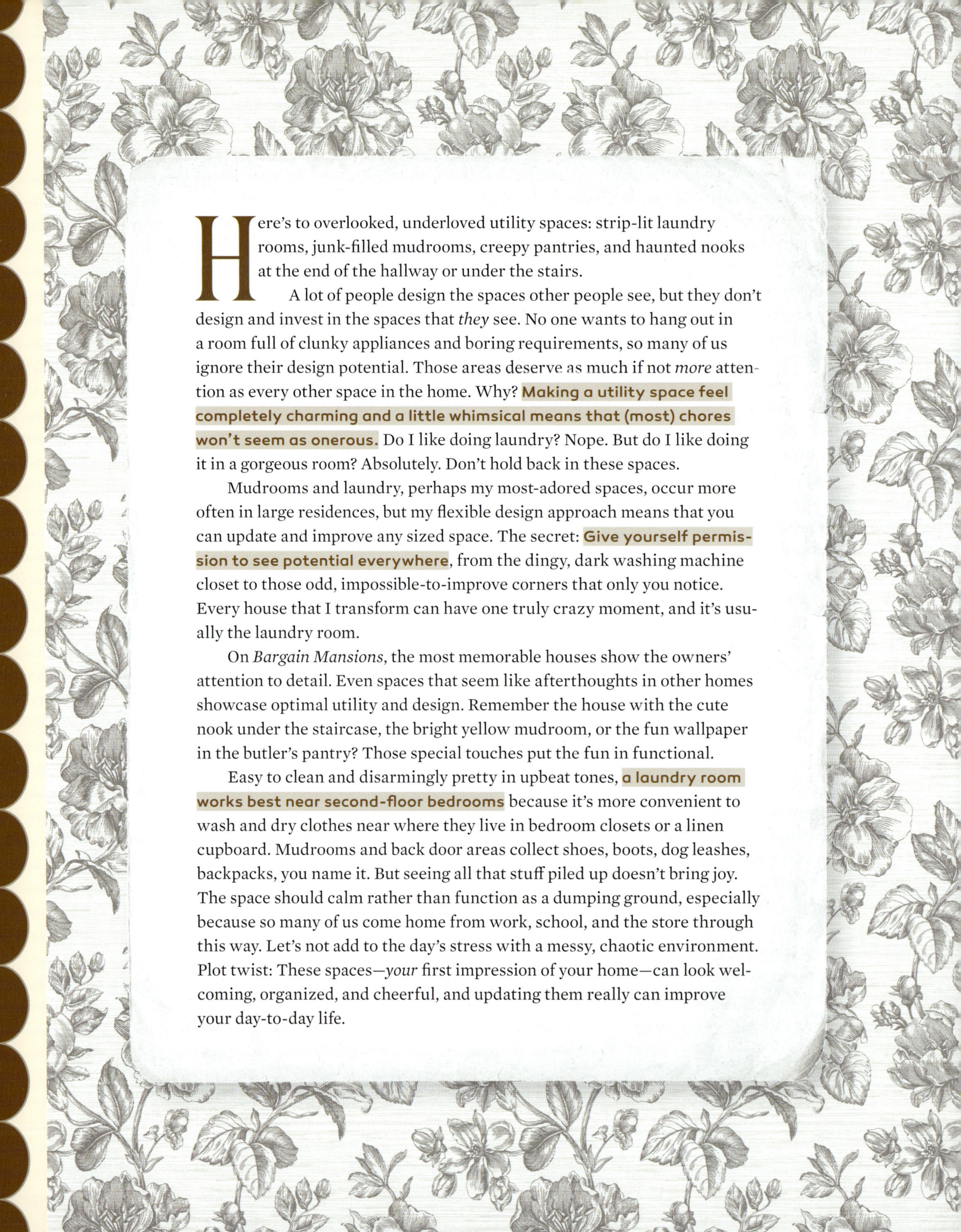

Here's to overlooked, underloved utility spaces: strip-lit laundry rooms, junk-filled mudrooms, creepy pantries, and haunted nooks at the end of the hallway or under the stairs.

A lot of people design the spaces other people see, but they don't design and invest in the spaces that *they* see. No one wants to hang out in a room full of clunky appliances and boring requirements, so many of us ignore their design potential. Those areas deserve as much if not *more* attention as every other space in the home. Why? **Making a utility space feel completely charming and a little whimsical means that (most) chores won't seem as onerous.** Do I like doing laundry? Nope. But do I like doing it in a gorgeous room? Absolutely. Don't hold back in these spaces.

Mudrooms and laundry, perhaps my most-adored spaces, occur more often in large residences, but my flexible design approach means that you can update and improve any sized space. The secret: **Give yourself permission to see potential everywhere**, from the dingy, dark washing machine closet to those odd, impossible-to-improve corners that only you notice. Every house that I transform can have one truly crazy moment, and it's usually the laundry room.

On *Bargain Mansions*, the most memorable houses show the owners' attention to detail. Even spaces that seem like afterthoughts in other homes showcase optimal utility and design. Remember the house with the cute nook under the staircase, the bright yellow mudroom, or the fun wallpaper in the butler's pantry? Those special touches put the fun in functional.

Easy to clean and disarmingly pretty in upbeat tones, **a laundry room works best near second-floor bedrooms** because it's more convenient to wash and dry clothes near where they live in bedroom closets or a linen cupboard. Mudrooms and back door areas collect shoes, boots, dog leashes, backpacks, you name it. But seeing all that stuff piled up doesn't bring joy. The space should calm rather than function as a dumping ground, especially because so many of us come home from work, school, and the store through this way. Let's not add to the day's stress with a messy, chaotic environment. Plot twist: These spaces—*your* first impression of your home—can look welcoming, organized, and cheerful, and updating them really can improve your day-to-day life.

COLORS

Let's Get Happy

Introduce color with bright wallpaper or water-resistant paint. Much as for a powder room (page 224), you can **make bolder choices in a mudroom or back hall**, since no one is spending tons of time in these spaces. You won't tire easily of dramatic design decisions as you might in other rooms. Lead with great-looking, "happy" colors: buttercup yellows, baby blues, and so on. If there's one room where I want you to feel confident in expressing your design personality, however out-there it might seem, it's here.

Oversized plaids and ginghams lend a cozy, farmhouse feel.

FLOORING

The Tough Stuff

Go for hardworking, scuffproof, stain-resistant, easy to clean, and fun to behold. Focus on water resistance to ensure that you can mop up spills or thrills. For both laundry and mudrooms, **tiling is my go-to here**; it looks great, and you can paint on a simple water-resistant coat after installation to super-power its waterproofing. Going vinyl is a good idea, but be careful with certain laundry products (bleach, some detergents), which can stain if left too long. Shop around for vinyl planks, some of which look remarkably woodlike, and look for sheet vinyl as an inexpensive alternative. Then dress it up with a rug. Speaking of rugs: If you're sorting clothes and ironing, **consider a squishy matt or washable rug** (or a rug over a mat or rug pad), to help with fatigue. Concrete, painted or etched, also works as a low-budget winner.

Muted herringbone tiles add to the lightness of this bright, calming space.

LIGHTING

Bright Ideas

These working spaces require a high level of light. **Add recessed, can lighting for brightness.** If you have the room, a statement pendant, decorative sconces, or both will look great and give your eyes a break. Oh, and maybe a chandelier (more on that later).

Bold wallpapers offer another way to surprise and delight.

A statement light for a laundry room? Why not?

LAYOUT

Making Your Space Work (Hard)

There's almost endless opportunity for function here. If you can, add cabinets, counters, or even an island with outlets to your laundry room. Large drawers and cabinets with pull-outs make life easier when hunting for detergent and other essentials. Again, if space allows, consider bar seating for sitting after an hour's folding and ironing.

If you're low on space, stack your washer and dryer. If both units sit side by side and load from the front, cap them with a counter for folding and staging. **The less you have to move clothes around, the easier they become to clean.** Add appliance pedestals for two great reasons: Each unit sits a little higher, making it easier to reach everything, saving your back in the process, and the pedestal can contain a cabinet for storing what you need. Don't forget to think about venting opportunities, too. Can you run a short vent outside, or will you be plumbing in a condensing dryer? What about a pocket door or curtains in a cute fabric to hide the units themselves? My laundry room has a slanted ceiling, but it still houses a pair of stacked washers and dryers (not excessive because four kids).

Does your dog love mud or water? Most of them do! If you have space and budget, think about installing a dog-washing station: a walk-in, half-height, tiled shower. My dog-loving clients *love* these. If your cat has access to your mudroom, consider rehoming the litter box in a cabinet here with a kitty-size opening cut into the door.

If your laundry area lives in a closet, walk-in or smaller, these tiny spaces also can transform beautifully into more functional, happier spaces by adding extra storage and a fold-out table or ironing board alongside a pretty light fitting and some fun wallpaper. In fact, an easy-to-clean counter space or even just a folding table makes it the perfect craft or art room for the kids—or you!

STORAGE SOLUTIONS

Overthink It

Under a bench that provides a place to sit and take off shoes, cubbies offer a place to store those shoes. Built-ins always look great, but big box and online home retailers sell easy flat-pack DIY cubbies. As with bathrooms (page 226), closed storage looks great in laundry spaces because essentials rarely match cohesively. Chances are that you have a hallway, unused corner, or nook nearby. Can you box it to create overflow storage?

Hooks work in more than just kids' bedrooms. On the wall of a back entry, they make hanging coats, jackets, leashes, and keys so much easier, and you don't have to fumble to find them. **Choose novelty or decorative hooks** instead of plain metal or wood. Mix and match.

Penny tiles come in sheets for speedy installation.

Home Stories

THE SUNSHINE COMBO

This combination laundry and mudroom had so much space to utilize. For the paintwork, is there a happier color than sunshine yellow? Wrapping the room in a beautiful graphic floral paper gave it a fun, almost cartoonish element, and trim work and windows in crisp white ensure that the cabinets hold center stage. The mini brick porcelain floor in black provides contrast and easy cleaning. **This is how you design happy.**

Paint color: Sherwin Williams Daffodil

A perfectly unexpected but useful place for a bar cart.

LUXURY LAUNDRY

This simple, functional take feels considered with a touch of whimsy. A little alcove holds the washer and dryer, and the workspace to the left works as a folding or craft space. Restoring the warm, honeyed-wood details in the old trim around the windows and crown molding and adding a delicate mural wallpaper with butterflies and branches lift the spirits while scrubbing collars. The best part: the hand-blown glass chandelier, yes, in a laundry room. **When a room looks this good, why not add a fabulous fixture?**

FUNCTIONAL AND FUN

This room originally formed part of a sunroom, full of period detail, such as the window frames and vintage radiator. In the redesign, it lost one set of windows, but natural light still floods the space and illuminates the dusty blue paintwork, graphic wallpaper, and gold hardware. The window seat and pillows nod to the space's past, and putting the hamper in cabinetry with portholes makes it fun to toss clothes into it.

BOLD COLOR

This mud space and laundry sat off the garage, so the dominant color needed to feel bold and invigorating. Electric blue paint looks perfect against the custom cabinetry with built-in bench seat and storage. Under the apron-front sink with black marble surround, spot the small, pull-out dog-feeding station. On the floor, hardworking hex tiles add calmness with a ruglike pattern in subtle tones of blue, white, and navy.

Storage and seating: mudroom essentials.

Paint color: Sherwin Williams Oceanside

SECRET DETAILS

This laundry space has a curious location. It sits off the main entryway, between the main bathroom and closet, at the bottom of the stairs that all the kids use, making it the most convenient placement for the whole family. The custom cabinets went sage green, with a Tahitian cream marble countertop and a tonal ceramic hex tile on the floor. Just behind the stacked washers and dryers, almost out of shot, sit two hampers on casters that the clients can access from the walk-in closet on the other side of the wall. Fill the hamper and push it through! The two sets of stackable washers and dryers come from my home's playbook. A pocket door allows for closing the space when guests arrive, but it looks so lovely in there that I'd keep it wide open.

* Enclosed storage keeps this walk-through space sleek and minimal.

Paint color: Farrow and Ball Pigeon

FOR THE LOVE OF DOGS

Once dysfunctional and small, this space had entryways to two garage spaces, a closet, laundry, and kitchen. It looked like a funhouse hall of doors, and not in a good way. That also meant no wall space to build anything, which had to change. Now a mudroom, it has a series of storage lockers, a little pull-up desk, and—because the clients have a cute little pooch—a dog-washing area that doubles as a boot-washing station, plus a water station with a pot filler, and room for a dog bed. The deep, bold colors and subway tiling of the dog-washing area set off the whole, multifunctional room, which looks fabulous.

Pro Tip

Design for everyone's needs, even your dog's. With so much time spent caring for our canines, a little thought here will make your post-walk routine 100 percent easier.

LOW COST, HIGH IMPACT

Storage cubes, boxes, and baskets prove incredibly useful in laundry and mudrooms. These baskets had a delightful graphic appeal, almost like a sunburst. They cost a song online and contrast beautifully with the custom cabinetry. The shiplap took on a deep, rich green-black, the same tone as the nearby kitchen, creating a color story in this fun, budget-friendly, easy-to-clean space.

THE WORLD'S SMALLEST LAUNDRY ROOM

In this house, rearranging the upstairs layout meant I was able to turn a tiny walk-in closet into this much-needed laundry room. The full bathroom sits close by, making the plumbing part of the job easy. This skinny custom cabinet added storage with butterfly wallpaper and color-matched paintwork in a rich green. The flooring tile pattern reflects the wonderful age of the house, and stackable washers of course saved space. I wanted this small space to be truly functional, feel considered, and look too pretty for words.

I wanted this small space to be truly functional, feel considered, and look too pretty for words.

CHECKLIST

- ☐ Go big with color for wallpapers or tiling in this highly personalized "hidden" space.
- ☐ Select hard-wearing, water-resistant flooring that matches your aesthetic.
- ☐ Keep lighting bright and functional with a little personality.
- ☐ Always have some form of counter space within reach.
- ☐ Use smart storage to transform these chaotic spaces.

11

BACKYARD SPACES

TAKE IT OUTSIDE

Before you learn my design secrets to backyard spaces, I'm going to say it. **If you have kids, you need a trampoline.** It's the single greatest investment you can make in this area. Ours spend more time on it than using or playing with any other backyard toy. It works like a magnet for friends, playdates, and developing social skills, and it burns off that crazy kiddo energy. Heck, even adults like to take a turn. It costs pennies per use—so worth it. If you have the room, get one, and to bounce it up a notch, make it a safer, in-ground model.

But back to the subject at hand. In Kansas, we enjoy the outdoors all year: tulip fields in spring, pumpkin patches in the fall, games at Arrowhead Stadium, and year-round barbecue festivals. (Kansas City 'cue is the best in the world. I won't be taking questions.) My own backyard serves many purposes, with lots of soft grass for sports; house-width, multilevel decks with a grill for those barbecues; pathways of pale pea gravel, stone, and pavers for strolling; retractable awnings; and comfortable seating for relaxing in nature.

But that's not all. When we moved in, our house looked like a wreck, including the backyard. Instead of fragrant flowers and colorful shrubbery, we had a swamp and feral cats. It took a lot of time to improve the space and make it really work for us. Over the years, it has seen a putting green, daybed swing, that in-ground trampoline, a 7-foot tube slide, and even an outdoor kitchen with a fire pit, smoker, and pizza oven. That tube slide, once adored by my kids and their friends, now does its duty more often for an adult at the end of an impromptu barbecue night, and I love that!

Backyards offer a great place for self-expression because their privacy affords more opportunities for creativity than the front yard, which can require a little more restraint, especially if your homeowners association has stringent rules. Like other, more utilitarian spaces indoors, these spaces come to life with a little design attention. Let your design imagination run wild.

these private outdoor spaces also mean fun!

Even if you don't have the budget or space to indulge in all these elements, many of them, including a DIY fire pit, a fragrant flower and herb garden, or a swing, probably lie within reach. Even small back gardens, terraces, and private balconies can incorporate more than one of these ideas.

Dress your deck in a bold outdoor rug to bring a little indoor luxe to your outside.

Thinking of making your backyard a little more fun? Jump to it!

LAYOUT

Sketch It Out

The function of the backyard or any private outside space has looser definition and rules than most other home spaces. Unless you're devoting the entire thing to food planting, **it should facilitate enjoyment, allow for a little al fresco living, and look pretty while doing it**. Do you crave a perfectly formal space with calming planting, stone pathways, and Zen detailing? A wild, back-to-nature forest with a fairy-tale pergola, a sports and fitness zone, a traditional English cottage garden, or a combination of everything you love?

Think in terms of layers: a border of taller shrubs and trees at the perimeter, for privacy, and other more ornamental plants and blooms, diminishing in height, closer to your home. Start by measuring your space, identify your needs (shade for summer, a covered spot for unpredictable weather), add the plants and details you love, and sketch your ideas.

A series of zones works best: a couple of seating areas, al fresco eating and kitchen area, room for games, a veggie patch, a swing. Consider the view from the house and the view from each sitting or eating zone. Make sure there's always something pretty to see. Remember that **it's a personal space and should work well for you and your loved ones**.

GREENSCAPING VERSUS HARDSCAPING

Mixing Soft and Strong

Start with the greenery, landscaping for color and texture, privacy and entertaining, fragrance and even food. Your greenscaping might include pollinator-friendly plantings (let's hear it for the bees), low-effort/high-impact grasses, grass alternatives, a summer salsa pot (page 18), and even low-maintenance, Zenlike rock areas.

From patios and walkways to walls and trellises, **hardscaping looks best when planned in relation to planting**. If you have a deck, style it just like an interior space with a rug, durable couch and chairs, even a pendant or floor lamp. For partial shade, add a pergola over a seating area. Pergolas look great and prove surprisingly useful for hanging pendant or market lights, ferns and other plants, or even paper pompoms. Add a vine or climbing plant to soften any otherwise sharp-edged garden structure.

FURNITURE

Lie-Back Luxe

On a deck, patio, or the lawn, supercomfortable seating provides a place to chill and hang while waiting for whatever's cooking on the grill. I love a weatherproof sectional, but **you have endless options from which to choose**: Adirondack chairs, woven loungers, waterproof wicker, wrought iron table and chairs, luxe daybeds with a draped (bugproof) canopy. Don't forget side tables for books and drinks. Don't feel shy about checking second-hand marketplaces, online or otherwise, for deals.

Add some stylish deck boxes, low coffee tables with storage underneath, and potting tables with drawers for storage. For the smallest spaces, a simple storage bench can house small rakes, seeds and secateurs, potting compost, bug spray, outdoor game equipment, or soft furnishings when sudden rainstorms hit. Consider parasols and sunshade sails in pretty fabrics. **Retractable canopies are worth every penny.** Dress your seating areas like interior spaces. Think rechargeable lamps, area rugs, and way too many pillows.

Laid-Back Lexicon

DECK USUALLY RAISED AND ATTACHED TO THE HOUSE

PATIO FLAT AND NOT ATTACHED TO THE HOUSE

PORCH COVERED ENTRANCE AT THE FRONT OF THE HOUSE

TERRACE LEVELED LAND NEXT TO THE HOUSE, PATIO, OR VERANDA

VERANDA COVERED GALLERY WRAPPING AROUND THE HOUSE

OUTDOOR KITCHEN

Summer fun isn't complete without grilling. My grill does its job almost all year long—that's how much I love cooking al fresco. **If you have the space and like to cook, a grill is a must**: a small, portable charcoal grill; a low-tech pizza oven; or a fixed monster with six burners and a smoker. Everyone can afford something, a cute tabletop Japanese yakitori grill, for example. An outdoor console made of cedar, treated lumber, or composite material provides a surface for serving delicious grub.

FIRESIDE

Light It Up

Fire pits create places to sit and enjoy warmth and ambience. Options range from inexpensive and DIY possibilities to more extravagant choices, which can include running a gas line to a stone fireplace or tabletop fireplace for instant flames whenever you want. Either way, a fire pit or firelight alternative can fit your budget or space restrictions. For burning natural wood, always use a spark arrestor and have a watering can nearby, for safety. S'mores are nonnegotiable.

Home Stories

LIVING IT UP OUTSIDE

Overlooked by the dining room, living room, and main bedroom, this backyard space feels like a collection of extra rooms: a fireside seating area, with the chimney wrapped in the same stone, a half wall to define the space, a new patio dining area, and a separate seating area. Iron ore–toned walls and copper downspouts give the area a unique appeal, but it really comes alive with accessories, warm-toned wood furniture, and a vase of blooms. A small water feature completed the trio of earth, wind, and fire.

Evenings by the outdoor hearth? Gimme s'more!

THE SLIM AARONS-LIKE POOL

If the name doesn't ring a bell, Slim Aarons photographed socialites living it big in gorgeous interiors and at the most glam pool parties. His work inspired the renovation of this luxurious pool, which hadn't seen an update in 50 years. Unfortunately, the original 1970s concrete elements had to go, but wrapping the entire deck with beautiful stone pavers completely transformed the space, as did adding little Astro-Turf "beach towels" under the elegant lawn chairs and restoring the original wrought iron furniture.

THE WORLD'S BIGGEST DECK

This huge backyard had a postage-stamp deck that was falling off the house. It became an enormous, ambitious living area and outdoor kitchen with grill, storage, and flat-top griddle—one of my favorite features in an outdoor kitchen. With it, you can boil stuff, make smash burgers, char your veggies, and never stink up your kitchen cooking bacon, fish, or mushrooms again. The new mini fridge has cottage detailing on the side. On the lower level, another seating area surrounds a fire pit. What can I say, we Kansans love being outdoors!

OUTDOOR LIVING ROOM

Under a deck, this secondary living area has a natural wood tongue-and-groove ceiling, light fixtures, and wall-mounted fans for breeze. Using composite decking material gave it a two-tiered effect, allowing it to become the family's outdoor living space, with a comfy sectional and coffee table. Again, **dress outdoor spaces the same as you would indoors**. Don't hold back with rugs, pillows, throws, and lanterns for lights.

A variation on the Adirondack chair—an American classic!

This pale natural wood lightened what was otherwise a low, dark space.

This polished stone inlay table adds a little laid-back luxe.

WHITEWASHING BAD DESIGN

The bones of this outdoor space held up nearly perfectly, but the colors looked dark and heavy, a product of the 1990s Tuscan craze. Everything desperately needed brightening, achieved by whitewashing the stone, giving the cabinetry a sleek contrast finish, and adding new countertops and three pendant lights.

ECLECTIC AND INSPIRED

This outdoor space feels quirky and inviting: vintage, eclectic, a little bohemian, and easy to do with a minimal budget. Cleaning up the little patio, painting the shed, and adding personality with a cluster of baskets took little time and effort. The custom fire pit started life as an old oil drum. Other charming details include the artful steel trellis and the beautiful horse tank pool, a stunning water feature on its own and a fun splash spot for the kids.

CHECKLIST

- ☐ Plan, plan, plan. Measure and sketch your ideas, incorporating as many vistas as possible.
- ☐ Add greenscaping *and* hardscaping rather than one or the other. Include something for the bees.
- ☐ Design your seating and eating areas like interior rooms, with side tables, a rug, and storage.
- ☐ Add fire as a focal point.
- ☐ Get yourself a grill, from a portable yakitori to a barbecue beast.

Acknowledgments

First and foremost, a huge thank-you to my house. You've been my most loyal and patient guinea pig for the past 16 years, enduring nonstop projects, from half-baked ideas to the full-blown "What have I gotten myself into?" endeavors. (If this house could talk, it probably would need therapy!) You're the birthplace of *Bargain Mansions*, the inspiration behind *Laid-Back Luxe*, and the keeper of a million memories—I wouldn't trade you for anything.

This home has been the place of countless celebrations and milestones: It's where we welcomed our greatest surprise, Eleanor, and it's where I've hosted everything from birthday parties and baby showers to engagement parties and graduations. It's seen a thousand (yes, a thousand) Connect Four tournaments at the kitchen table, countless forced rounds of Rummikub with the family, and cozy snuggles by the fire. These memories I cherish most—the ones that make it all worthwhile.

To my wonderful husband, Bill: Thank you for being the eternal optimist, the life of the party, and the one who pulls me out of my introverted ways. You always are willing to dive in to one project after another with the belief that somehow it all will work out. (You may deserve a medal or at least a nice, quiet vacation.) Thank you for being by my side for the last 25 years. We have a lot more memories to create together. I can't wait to see what's next. I love you.

To my kids, Henry, Bobby, Thomas, and Eleanor: You've lived through more dust, noise, and chaos than any child should reasonably endure. Thank you for your patience, your resilience, and your ability to survive yet another dinner party with a side of drywall. You are the lights of my life, and when I look at our home, I see 16 years of memories with you at the center of them all. Our house is never better than when you all are here with me. I'm so proud of each of you in so many ways, but mostly I'm proud of your hearts. My daily prayer for each of you is this: "Lord, please keep my children's mind, body, and spirit safe. Protect their steps as they leave our home and let them lead others with kindness and wisdom from You. Thank You for these precious lives that I get to be a part of and let them know they are adored by me and You, unconditionally."

To Dad (aka Ward): Thank you for showing up to those first few days of filming to make sure everything was going well and to ensure that I wasn't being scammed—and for being such a character that they had to put you on screen. Thank you for showing up season after season when you'd rather have been at the farm. Thank you for being the funny to my serious, for teaching me to figure it out as I go, that there's nothing I can't figure out (math not included), for teaching me everything I know—and sometimes even letting me teach you a thing or two.

To my mom, the ultimate mom: Thank you for being the foundation of faith in our home and teaching us to care deeply for others, for being home with something homemade, healthy, and usually delicious (unless carob was involved) every day after school. You were always ready to hear all my stories, and you still are. You hide when the cameras come out, but you're my silent supporter hiding in the wings, my spa-junkie partner in crime, always up for a massage after a hard day of demo, and I still can count on something yummy and homemade every time I come home to you.

To my brothers, Ben and Caleb: Thank you, Ben, for being in the hardware store 15 years ago when a casting person approached you, only for you to pass on it and suggest our woodworking guru brother, Caleb, who said, "Hey, my sister does some cool house stuff." Without two cute brothers who (most of the time) actually like me, I wouldn't be writing this book, and *Bargain Mansions* wouldn't exist. Thank you, both, for letting me shine. Caleb, thank you for raising two great girls, Abigail and Andee Claire. Andee Claire is Eleanor's "big sister," and her faith and influence in Eleanor's life will be with her forever. She's a great example of a beautiful, strong, independent woman who I know Eleanor aspires to be. Ben (again!), thank you for letting Jami and me take over your annual NYC tennis trip to go shopping and be inspired in the city—and to you both for being my forever Monday-night TV-watching sounding board.

To my sister, Sara: You're a constant encourager and endless supporter of my dreams, always believing that I can do more than I believe I can. Thank you for praying over every part of this path and being the best aunt in the world to my kids, pouring your time and love into them. I'm so thankful they have you to run to when life gets hard. Your ability to listen and empathize is unmatched. I'm so glad I prayed and prayed for a little sister. You're everything I prayed for. Thanks to you and Nate for trusting me with your own home, and thank you for the five-chip chocolate chip cookies and for always being a call away when we need you for a quick three-hour design session.

To Beth: You've been doing this mom life with me for the last 21 years and have made space for the ups and downs of proud-mom moments and mom-guilt moments alike. I couldn't—and wouldn't—want to do it without you. Someday, we'll be nursing home besties.

To Matt Antrim, creator of *Bargain Mansions*: I was pretty sure you were a "you could be a model" scam, but it turns out that you actually know your stuff. I forever will wonder what made you think, *She'd make great TV!* Your humor and ability to make me "Sparkle, darling, sparkle" every day are appreciated endlessly.

To Colin Whelan, owner of Conveyor Media and producer of *Bargain Mansions*: Thank you for investing blood, sweat, and a few actual tears over the years. Thank you for assembling such an incredibly talented team in Lauren Brady, Cortney Hopkins, Kassidy Sell, Chad Swenson, Ty Jones, Super Steve Frasher, Mary Anne Churchill, Anastasia Rendina, and the many more whom I can't fit in this space. Like I tell every nervous homeowner, your entire job is to make us look good. Despite the chaos and occasional mess (OK, fine, *often* a mess), you still make it all look perfect.

To Loren Ruch: Without your friendship and belief in *Bargain Mansions*, this would've remained nothing more than a dream. You've supported us from *Little Money Mansions* to DIY Network, HGTV, Magnolia Network, and Max. We're the little show that could, and we've made it together. I am endlessly grateful to you.

To the Scripts Network, DIY Network, HGTV, Chip and Joanna Gaines, Magnolia Network, and Max: *Wow.* I never could've dreamed that *Bargain Mansions* would thrive on so many platforms and continue to be reinvented. Thank you for the platform that has made my dreams come true.

To my tiny but incredibly mighty Tamara Day Team . . .

Denise Cadenas: Thank you for being by my side through the ups and downs of life, for encouraging all my "bad" habits because we share them, and for always being there when I have a design dilemma and can't make up my mind! You have helped build this dream with me from the very beginning. Thank you! I'm so grateful for that "blind date" that your mom set us up on 18 years ago. She just knew we'd be instant friends. (Thank you, Stella!)

Livi Abney: Thank you for telling me that I was wrong before we even met via email! Your boldness and ability to tell me there's another way to look at situations—and continue to push me, even when I don't want to be pushed—are forever appreciated. Thank you for being a truth-teller and leader of our pack, for indulging my often-wild ideas, for helping build this dream behind the scenes, and for being a friend through it all.

Olivia Thomas: Thank you for being the best intern I've ever hired! You're the actual best cheerleader. Your endless energy, belief in everything that I suggest, and willingness to work crazy hours while always smiling are priceless. This book wouldn't exist without your detailed eye and understanding of my crazy mind. You really can read my mind and execute better than I ever could on the million details of this book! Thank you for being *you*.

To all our photographers: You capture the good, the bad, and the ugly! When I look back at the furniture-painting days in the driveway, I think, *Why didn't I take more photos, and why are they all so bad?!* Photographer, I am not! It always blows my mind that I can take the same photo from the same spot but your magic makes mine look like an iPhone 2.0, while yours look next level. Thank you for walking through the scary befores and even some of the sweltering hot or freezing cold afters! Thank you for making my five photo poses look fresh and original and for laughing all the way through those hectic days!

To Roger Behle: Thank you for supporting my vision for this book and introducing me to Todd Shuster at Aevitas, who understood what I wanted to create and helped bring Jack Haug and Dan Jones on board to make this vision a reality.

To Dan: You are an endless smile! Every time we talk, you bring out the best version of me, and you somehow have brought my ideas, experiences, and voice to life. I can't imagine that there's anyone better suited to help craft this book, and I'm forever grateful for your enthusiasm and dedication to the words and the process. You are one of a kind, my friend!

To Jenna Kaufmann: You were there in the beginning of this crazy ride and helped to bring this dream into reality. Thank you for everything.

To the team at Countryman Press: James Jayo, thank you for your patience in putting the proposal together in the most perfect way that has made this book a reality. Your expert input has helped shape and refine it into what it is today. Allison Chi, you've been a delight to get to know. Seeing the creativity, color, whimsy, and charm that I always hoped for come to life is because of your excitement for this book. I can't wait to have that glass of wine together and learn to spin wool with you!

I especially thank the homeowners who have trusted me with this crazy process over the years. Thank you for letting me push your limits in design just a little further and loving it all. This book wouldn't exist without your spaces. I cherish the friendships that have been created along the way, and it brings me so much joy to see your families living and loving in the homes I've had the privilege of shaping. Thank you for the gift of letting me be a small part of your story.

Finally, to Kansas City: Thank you for being the big city with bright lights and small-town charm. I've built my business here, raised my family here, and celebrated most of my grown-up wins here. I often say that even though Dad is my costar, KC is the true star of the show. I am so proud to share all that our incredible city has to offer. Go Chiefs!

Love,
Tamara
X

Product Index

1. Quorum Veno 8-Light Ceiling Mount—Aged Brass

1. Tamara Day for Quorum Bonnel 20" Pendant—Matte Black; 2. Lee Boulevard 8-Light Chandelier—Matte Black; 3. Belinder 4-Light Pendant—Aged Brass; 4. LOIRE 8-Light Pendant—Matte Black/Brushed Brass

1. Tamara Day for Varaluz Swiss Wall 50" Mirror—Dark Blue; 2. Farra 36" Mirror—Poplar Burl; 3. Carlton 33" Mirror—Gold; 4. Scallop 54" Mirror

1. Tamara Day for Stylecraft Celeste Blush Gold Pure Crystal Table Lamp; 2. Tamara Day for Quorum Charlotte-8 Light Chandelier—Aged Brass

1. Tamara Day for Stylecraft Patchwork—Peonies; 2. —Applescape; 3. —Blush Horizon; 4. —Mauve Fields

1. Tamara Day by Spectra Home Meyer Chair; 2. Tamara Day by Spectra Home Dearborn Sofa

1. Tamara Day by Spectra Home Mackey Sectional; 2. Tamara Day by Spectra Home Olivia Sofa; 3. Tamara Day for Stylecraft Scallop-Edged Pillow 206; 4. Tamara Day for Stylecraft Scallop-Edged Pillow 221

1. Cyan Design Estrella Pendant—Black

1. Tamara Day by Spectra Home Sagamore Sofa; 2. Tamara Day for Stylecraft Belinda Stone Table Lamp; 3. Edmund Pearl Blush Ceramic Table Lamp

1. Tamara Day for Quorum Charlotte 3-Light Wall Mount—Matte Black; 2. Cyan Design Ravello Pendant; 3. York Wallcoverings Juniper Forest Wallpaper

1. Tamara Day for RoomMates Botanical Garden Wallpaper—Greens

1. Front & Center Fineline Door Front

1. Mersea Palermo Linen Embroidered Top

1. Daltile Revalia Remix Tile; 2. Quorum Soft Contemporary Globe Pendant—Black and Aged Brass

1. Quorum Marquee 6-Light Pendant; 2. Quorum One-Light Two-Toned Wall Mount—Black and Aged Brass

1. Tamara Day by Spectra Home—Shenandoah Stone Fabric 2. —Kalahara Saxony Fabric 3. —Navigator Mineral Fabric 4. —Tilly Domino Fabric

1. Tamara Day by Spectra Home Buena Vista Swivel Chair; 2. Tamara Day by Spectra Home Woodson Chair; 3. Tamara Day for Stylecraft Beatrice Pure Crystal Glass Accent Lamp—Burgundy; 4. Verena Steel Table Lamp

1. Tamara Day for Quorum Lee Boulevard 5-Light Bead Chandelier—Matte Black; 2. Tamara Day by Spectra Home Hadley Chair

1. Tamara Day by Spectra Home Locust Cocktail Ottoman

1. Tamara Day for Quorum Belleview 8-Light Pendant

1. York Wallcoverings Kaleidescope Wallpaper

1. Tamara Day for Varaluz Carlton 33" Mirror—Gold; 2. Energy Pro Windows and Siding

1. Quorum Vertigo Chandelier

1. Tamara Day for Varaluz Carlton 33" Mirror—Chrome

1. Uttermost Crossing Small Bench; 2. Tamara Day by Spectra Home Woodward Swivel Chair

1. York Wallcoverings Botanical Fantasy Wallpaper

1. Tamara Day for Quorum Charlotte-5 Light Chandelier—Matte Black

1. Tamara Day for Varaluz Not Baroque-en 40" Mirror—Gold

1. Tamara Day for Quorum Mercier 2-Light Wall Mount—Matte Black

1. York Wallcoverings Peacock Block Print Wallpaper

1. Tamara Day for Varaluz Carlton 33" Mirror—Gold; 2. Tamara Day for Quorum Charlotte 1-Light Wall Mount—Aged Brass

1. Quorum Piazza 14" Indoor/Outdoor Wall Fan—Black

1. Tamara Day for Stylecraft Verity Brass Table Lamp Formica Shade

General Index

D

E

F

G

H

I

J

K

V

W

Y